PRAISE FOR *CHURCH FINANC*
BEST PRACTICES FOR

"*Church Finances for Missional Leaders* is packed with guidelines, tools, worksheets, and strategies that will help pastors and lay leadership better understand terminology and best principles and practices for giving and stewarding. You'll refer to this book again and again as you encourage faithful generosity in your congregation all year long."

—**Marcia Shetler**, executive director/CEO, Ecumenical Stewardship Center

"Wow. This is the useful and comprehensive 'textbook' offering a 360-degree approach to local church finances for congregations of all sizes. From cover to cover, this book includes practical church financial management and stewardship information, templates to customize, and useful guidance for finance, stewardship, and trustee committees, pastors and treasurers.

—**Sheri M. Altland**, United Methodist Communications Foundation, and UMC Campaign Director for Imagine No Malaria

"Pastors and lay leaders will benefit greatly from this fine, new resource! Bonnie Marden has given stewardship committees a book to read, pastors a reference work to consult, and lay leaders an imaginative collection to study. Here is help for missional leaders, looking for best practices in stewardship. What shines through the whole book is a sense of gratitude, of goodness, and of generosity, all of which bring inspiration and encouragement."

—**Robert Allan Hill**, dean of Marsh Chapel, Boston University

CHURCH FINANCES FOR MISSIONAL LEADERS

BEST PRACTICES FOR FAITHFUL STEWARDSHIP

BONNIE IVES MARDEN

Church Finances for Missional Leaders: Best Practices for Faithful Stewardship

The General Board of Higher Education and Ministry leads and serves The United Methodist Church in the recruitment, preparation, nurture, education, and support of Christian leaders—lay and clergy—for the work of making disciples of Jesus Christ for the transformation of the world. The General Board of Higher Education and Ministry of The United Methodist Church serves as an advocate for the intellectual life of the church. The Board's mission embodies the Wesleyan tradition of commitment to the education of laypersons and ordained persons by providing access to higher education for all persons.

The Wesley's Foundery Books is an imprint of the General Board of Higher Education and Ministry, The United Methodist Church, and named for the abandoned foundery that early followers of John Wesley transformed, which became the cradle of London's Methodist movement.

Church Finances for Missional Leaders: Best Practices for Faithful Stewardship

Disclaimer: Legal and tax policies are subject to changes. Always seek legal counsel or tax professional advice to confirm current regulations and policies. This information is intended to be informative and educational only.

All web addresses were correct and operational at the time of publication.

ISBN 978-1-945935-42-8

19 20 21 22 23 24 25 26 27 28—10 9 8 7 6 5 4 3 2 1

Manufactured in the United States of America

CONTENTS

ACKNOWLEDGMENTS

People have trusted and blessed me for as long as I can remember with their stories, questions, and hopes, often including visions for successful financial stewardship to fund missions. Their willingness to share their hopes and ideas has inspired and encouraged me over the years. As an organizational consultant and financial campaign coordinator, I have journeyed with leaders working through challenges and even conflict created by financial issues. I have also witnessed the joy of successful campaigns and financial miracles. Many have asked when this knowledge would be shared; I am grateful for your patience.

This book also benefitted from opportunities gained through experiences with the United Methodist Foundation of New England and the UMC Initiative to Address Economic Challenges Facing Pastoral Leaders. Working with these organizations confirmed my belief that many of us need a basic financial stewardship workbook to build confidence and courage for this leadership responsibility. My respect for the complexity of stewardship—technically, professionally, and spiritually—has also greatly increased.

Many congregations served as study labs for the materials in this book, and I thank all who allowed me to teach, learn, and develop these resources with them. Preaching and consulting invitations have created space to explore the spiritual dimensions of this calling and to dialogue with national leaders about giving and generosity, donor relations, socially responsible investments, and financial accountability and integrity. Launching MYTE^4 Ministries has allowed this work to become a calling to Multiply Yahweh's Treasures Efficiently, Effectively, Enthusiastically for Everyone. I pray this becomes a community where generosity is reclaimed as a spiritual discipline (rather than a result of good stewardship), new voices are elevated and donor appreciation is our top priority.

My overflowing gratitude includes awareness of the presence of my parents, Cliff and Jane, who taught me important stewardship principles about integrity and generosity and allowed me to find my call in my own unique way. For all who have shared ideas and insights, I hope you see the contribution you have made to this book. Special thanks to Steve Garnaas-Holmes, who shared his poetic stewardship visions included as multiple epigraphs.

I am so grateful and blessed by past and present champions who have learned and grown with me; you are co-creators of this gift.

> The God who makes all things possible planted seeds;
> Your encouragement nurtured this into reality
> And I pray the fruits are plentiful and life-giving. Amen.

Bonnie Ives Marden
bonnie@myteministries.org

INVITATION

BECOME A COURAGEOUS STEWARD

Well done, good and faithful servant! You have been faithful with a few things; I will put you in charge of many things. Come and share your master's happiness!

—Matthew 25:23

Because you care about God's mission, you are a steward. As we navigate challenges to society's confidence in the integrity and financial accountability of faith communities, the world cries out for courageous leaders who take responsibility for restoring trust—for stewards. Appearing in eleventh-century manuscripts, the word *steward* comes from Greek and Hebrew roots—*stig* (meaning an enclosure or hall) and *wéord* (the trusted manager of the household's well-being).[1] While managing resources, sacred buildings, and assets continues to grow increasingly complicated, the steward's role as trusted caregiver remains clear. A steward manages another's possessions. A biblical steward acknowledges God's ownership and generosity; today, many parents' encouragement to *leave places better than when*

1 Douglas J. Hall, *The Steward: A Biblical Symbol Come of Age*, rev. ed. (Eugene, OR: Wipf and Stock Publishers, 2004), 40 and footnote.

you arrived echoes this expectation of stewards. This book explores financial stewardship responsibilities and offers tools for good and faithful servant leadership so that we all may share in furthering God's purposes.

Matthew 25:14-30 tell us that when the steward delivered ten talents to the master, he demonstrated ingenuity by doubling the five talents he had originally received. His skills multiplied the resources and earned him praise and trust. Similarly, the skills necessary to cultivate generosity and multiply money for mission includes confidence and knowledge about basic financial practices for accountability to God, donors, and our legal responsibilities. Stewards understand how money can inspire wise stewardship or invite unhealthy decisions, how financial reports inform or distort information, and how asking others to join our mission holds the possibility for changing the world. We need spiritual disciplines about money as well as financial management skills because having knowledge about finances doesn't always lead to faithful stewardship practices. A mission with $100 in the bank could be experiencing good stewardship or frightening vulnerability, while $100,000 may have similar meanings in other organizations. Good stewardship and financial security may have some common qualities; however, the norms and financial expectations of missional enterprises are quite diverse. Reclaiming the biblical and spiritual relationship between money and mission continues to be a great challenge—and opportunity.

Money and Mission

Stewardship encompasses more than managing money. In United Methodist churches, our membership vows include expressing our faith in Jesus Christ, our discipleship, by supporting the church's mission through five stewardship practices: prayer, presence, gifts, service, and witness.[2] The purpose of this book, building on this fact, is to equip leaders for financial stewardship of monetary gifts for missions. I am mindful of the Scripture: "From everyone who has been given much, much will be demanded; and from the one who has been entrusted with much, much more will be asked" (Luke 12:48b). We have been

---

2 From "Care of Members," *The Book of Discipline of The United Methodist Church: 2016* (Nashville, TN: The United Methodist Publishing House, 2016), ¶228.1.

given much indeed, and God's generosity can inspire us to lead stewardship holistically and increase our financial knowledge and skills. Financial stewardship requires deep reflection on our relationship with money. Sometimes we need to be confronted, confess our shortcomings, and change our behavior.

Without vision, people perish; without money, mission withers. The relationship between money and mission shapes and is shaped by a community's understanding of God's vision for humanity. Our relationship with money is complicated, triggering a range of attitudes and behaviors. Leaders must embrace the power and temptation of money for some people and implement appropriate safeguards. While Ananias and Sapphira's deadly consequences for withholding some of their gifts (Acts 5:1-11) are quite punitive, many people face similar temptation daily. Many of Jesus' parables involve money, including the Prodigal Son (Luke 15:18-32) and the man whose life was claimed by God the very night he finished building barns to hold his many possessions (Luke 12:16-21). Jesus talked boldly about greed, needless spending, and hoarding. The biblical antidote for an unhealthy relationship with money is generosity, along with disciplines and organizational policies that set clear expectations about financial reserves, debt, endowments, and check-signing procedures.

Best practices are a safeguard against temptation and misconduct. My personal call to financial stewardship began when a beloved pastor's check-writing privileges proved to be insufficient protection from temptation. This tragedy could have been prevented if proper procedures had been in place. Church leaders and pastors need to implement financial best practices in order to prevent unwarranted temptation. Disciplined procedures for handling money also bolster the church's mission by nurturing transparency, and that, in turn, will inspire donors' and congregants' trust, thus amplifying the vision and mission!

Whether your church handles thousands of dollars or scrapes by month to month, stewardship decisions occur constantly. Deciding whether to alert everyone when summer income exceeds expectations or when dipping into reserves is required are stewardship dilemmas. The point at which bank account balances trigger anxiety varies widely based on cultural norms and history. Saving for future expenses, such as pastoral moving expenses, new music for the choir, or roof repairs, shows financial planning priorities. One group will courageously confront an unexpected boiler failure, costing thousands of dollars;

others will panic about much smaller but necessary termite treatment bills. How pastors and church leaders interact with leading donors reflects the stewardship culture and impacts missional capacity. And, leaders need to keep up with changes in tax policies and legal issues that affect charitable gifts.

In some cases, rather than speaking the truth about the absence of a compelling vision and mission, leaders unwisely spend thousands of endowment dollars propping up current expenses. The rigorous way that leaders debate financial decisions confirms the power and influence of money in faith communities. Let me assure you: all aspects of your mission are impacted by stewardship decisions as well as congregational attitudes toward money, which can be healthy or unhealthy but most likely are a mixture of both.

What do pastors do when their professional education includes little or no financial training? What should church leaders know about accounting? What should happen when expenses consistently exceed financial resources? How are unhealthy financial practices addressed when leaders are uncomfortable with accountability? What does God require of us? This book responds to these questions by presenting foundational financial concepts and stewardship principles so that pastors and leaders can better understand how money affects the church's success and missional leadership. Financial stewardship best practices come in handy whether you are trying to get funds deposited promptly, intelligently explaining the difference between designated and restricted funds, or deciding whether to invest or spend a surprise bequest gift. Leaders need to confidently and competently understand viable options in helpful ways, and they need to know enough of the language of finance to discuss their needs with professional consultants, accountants, or financial advisors. The descriptions, definitions, and worksheets in this book will build your confidence as financial leaders and help your church become more financially literate with the intent of furthering God's mission and purpose. These skills will also reduce the risks and consequences of not paying enough attention to financial procedures and practices, because too many congregations have experienced the painful consequences of

- unexpected bequests triggering fights (for example, between advocates for new missions, trustees demanding roof repairs, and influential members asking for additional ministry staff);

- pastors borrowing money from parishioners or from discretionary funds, intending to pay it back as soon as possible; or
- church leaders assuming a designated fund should be liquidated during a merger or being unaware of the tax implications of distributing scholarship funds to their children.

These incidents and others like them are prevented by accountable stewardship practices and knowledge.

Call to Confession

Our cultural avoidance of open, honest talk about money still challenges pastors and laity. Even if eager for financial knowledge, some readers will still feel uncomfortable talking about money. Worrying that people will find financial information distasteful allows our anxieties about money to hold us hostage. It allows money to control us rather than letting God direct our financial choices. Unfortunately, reluctance to talk about money is counterproductive because our fear can accelerate church decline and increase challenges leaders want to avoid. We are quick to describe money as evil, even though the Scripture text defines the *love* of money as the source of trouble (1 Tim. 6:10). Trouble arises, not because we have money, but because of our emotional relationship with money.

Jesus spoke consistently about money, possessions, and temptations, demonstrating his awareness of our vulnerability to their power to prevent us from living joyfully and generously as God intended. We relate to the young ruler, hoping his acts of kindness and mercy would earn him a place of honor. We also empathize with the young ruler's choice to return to his passions and possessions rather than to sell them all for the poor (Luke 18:18-24). John Wesley, founder of the Methodist movement, also wrote warnings about the use of money.[3] In his own life, Wesley practiced self-discipline with the money he earned, increasing his giving as his income grew. He also demonstrated the complexity of financial stewardship by purchasing an expensive

3 See John Wesley, "Sermon 50," in *The Use of Money*, ed. Thomas Jackson (1872), http://www.umcmission.org/Find-Resources/John-Wesley-Sermons/Sermon-50-The-Use-of-Money.

longer-lasting coat rather than a cheaper garment.[4] Sharing more openly about money and its role in our lives, as Wesley did, can affect our responses to questions like: *How much is enough? When do we feel secure enough to give it all away?*

Professionally, effective pastoral leadership requires financial knowledge. A pastor's leadership and the missional capacity of the church depend on commitment to a life of stewardship, which includes talking about money, even from the pulpit. Believing ministry is a profession where leaders avoid the topic of money limits pastoral effectiveness and mission outreach. If you need to reframe your relationship with money and its role in your life, or aren't convinced you are able to learn these skills, consider this testimonial:

> I want to share something remarkable and, for me, a real learning curve regarding donors. As suggested, I approached a generous couple and invited them to prayerfully consider a significant gift to a mission project. To be honest, these folks don't live extravagantly. So, I thought, they probably don't have much, and I don't want them to feel pressured. Then, yesterday, our financial secretary approached me before worship, gushing with excitement. The couple made a generous gift and she suggested we use it for church bills.
>
> Since this couple had supported our discretionary fund before, it occurred to me they may intend this gift for community needs rather than for our bills. Turns out, the check specifically said "benevolence." Before my arrival, benevolence checks were cashed and tucked somewhere in the financial secretary's house until the pastor called regarding a discretionary need. When I learned the discretionary money was at her home, I explained that we now have a discretionary funds bank account. I went to her house to drive her with the money to the bank. When I arrived, I found cash all over her kitchen table—the discretionary money she'd been saving for years.
>
> The donor's gift? In a sweet personal note to me, the couple invited us to use their $2,000 gift to help people in the community during the winter. The cash on the kitchen table? Total: $3,130. The financial secretary asked me one question as we drove

4 As told by Rev. Linda Campbell-Marshall, quoting a docent at Wesley's City Road Home in London.

to the bank: "Didn't I trust her?" I replied, "Yes, I do. We are putting this money in the bank because it is safer for you and for me and for the church. I'm going to send the couple a nice note. I'm going to visit them personally, and let them know about our mission projects." Wow, learning curve adjusted. Feels a little awkward, but I'll grow into it.

Blessings,
A Courageous Pastor

Financial Stewardship's Impact on Mission

Financial stewardship directly influences our mission because money fuels our missional activities, spreading God's love and Jesus' compassion to all the world. Through the best practices of financial stewardship, leaders shape our culture of generosity or of scarcity, which in turn affects our ministry capacity. Co-existing with financial experts and penny pinchers in their communities, pastors and finance leaders manage, interpret, and generate mission dollars. For faithful stewards, money's purpose *is* mission. In fact, without a clear connection to mission, money is only a tool for commerce rather than a vehicle for changing lives. The best mission activities mirror Jesus' life by focusing on serving others. Wise use of money increases its impact and value for the giver, for the recipient, and for the world. Therefore, effective leaders invest in their knowledge about financial management.

Which of the topics below are components of financial management and stewardship?

Communication
Accountability
Record-keeping
Asset Management
Budgeting
Planned Giving
Counting
Job Descriptions
Volunteer Coordination
Training/Orientation
Property Management

If you didn't choose all of them, review the list again.

Financial stewardship also encompasses leaders' influence on the morale and self-image of faith communities. When conversations about financial matters are strained or nonexistent, people notice. On the one hand, open dialogue increases ownership and reduces the risks that silence creates for individuals and missions. Clarity about roles and responsibilities creates healthy boundaries and support systems. It might even free the pastor and church treasurer from sleepless nights. On the other hand, asking staff or a pastor to "wait a few more days" before cashing their paychecks doesn't build trust or good will. God invites us to disrupt our culture's anxiety about money by practicing faith-based, financial stewardship to strengthen generosity and mission capacity. God deserves nothing less than our best.

 ***Prayer Pause***: What is more important: faith or money? 

Financial Management Is a Spiritual Discipline

Financial stewardship supports faith formation and cultivates money for mission. Stewards must fulfill our fiscal accountability such as paying payroll taxes *and* practice spiritual disciplines such as praying over the weekly offering and encouraging tithing. The faith-based perspective that God will provide and the practical tasks of paying bills create natural tensions, especially when the budget is underfunded. Differing perspectives emerge when we ask:

- Does financial security lie in prayer or pledges?
- Is financial security necessary for missional organizations?
- Is the chicken dinner's purpose to share the love of Jesus Christ with our neighbors or to fund the heating bill?

 Spiritual grounding and fiscal accountability are equally important to mission. 

Spiritual grounding and fiscal accountability are equally important to our missions. They cannot be separated; spiritual growth leads to greater financial accountability while increases in financial stewardship and generosity contribute to spiritual growth. If leaders suggest spiritual disciplines are more important than accountability or that finances are more significant than faith, they create lose-lose situations.

Managing finances and promoting generosity requires a *both/and* perspective. Polarity management,[5] a framework for *both/and* thinking, identifies

5 Barry Maxwell, *Polarity Management: Identifying and Managing Unsolvable Problems* (Amherst, MA: HRD Press, Inc.), 21–23.

interdependent opposites that create paired dynamics, requiring management rather than solutions. Barry Maxwell's examples include the *breathing in* and *breathing out* polarity, which manages lung functioning and life. Both inhaling and exhaling sustain life. Similarly, the financial stewardship of money for mission requires both spiritual discipline and practical skill. While specific disciplines or skills may be more important at certain times, insisting one is more valuable or biblical than the other leads very predictably to trouble. That is why the practical information in this book addresses spiritually grounded financial stewardship.

Proclamation of Mission Growth through Financial Stewardship

Financial behaviors by pastors and leaders affect mission capacity! When leaders celebrate what God is making possible, morale and mission capacity grow. When the breakfast fundraiser invites free-will donations rather than charging each person $2.25, generosity increases as attendees contribute $5, $10, or $20. I promise this works. When information about mission projects are shared during community fairs, festivals, or parades, or with shared users of our property, new partnerships emerge and mission grows. When narrative budget presentations convert spreadsheets into inspirational stories—with more visually appealing pie charts—giving, morale, and confidence increase. Our financial behaviors and procedures impact generosity.

Rather than limiting mission to a specific budget line-item, what if we identify everything as mission? When every dollar clearly supports mission, giving grows. Many faith communities host community and support groups, influencing the lives of people we may never see but who benefit from our spaces and affect our neighborhoods. Our missions and financial activities with businesses such as florists, printers, and local restaurants bless the local community and economy, especially when we pay bills on time. Having a healthy reputation in the community and with local businesses may even inspire generosity, such as discounts for property repairs, fuel, or even cleaning supplies! Our community mission through our financial transactions is significantly greater than our budget suggests. Every financial transaction is an act of stewardship and mission.

People respond generously to human need, less so to institutions. Let's clearly identify ourselves as a faith community that serves people. When every expenditure is missional, we see the benefits and impact of our giving more clearly. Roof repairs are as valuable as food-pantry donations when spiritual growth and healing take place under that roof. When our mind-set is that all aspects of ministry are missional, our stewardship of the gifts people share from the resources God has given them becomes sacred work: ministry.

This book equips you to order the financial life of your church's missional endeavors. Grounded in a biblical understanding of the steward's role, the vocabulary, definitions, responsibilities, resources, and worksheets will equip leaders for the stewardship of money for mission. While one dollar always represents one hundred pennies, other aspects of finances and financial management will change. Best practices, rules, and laws affecting financial stewardship will experience minor adjustments or major revisions. Despite inevitable changes, this practical resource will help leaders talk about money, even leaders who find this uncomfortable. Let's remove the barrier to joyful, life-giving ministry and become courageous stewards. I pray also for faithful accountability to one another, to God, and to the communities who know us as agents of mission.

Numerous stewardship advocates have packaged financial stewardship information in evolving formats, courageously challenging cultural norms about money and missions and celebrating our gratitude to God. This is not meant to be your last stewardship book, but it should be one of your first, a resource to return to as needed. This book addresses topics and principles from many stewardship resources, validating their usefulness and continuing relevance for leaders. I have integrated those that are most helpful with additional financial content to equip you for confident and courageous stewardship leadership, moving beyond diagnosis of the changes needed to practical, culture-shifting actions.

When using this collection of practical tools for financial stewardship, you may want to browse for a specific topic or work through each section for a comprehensive overview. Regulations affecting financial management vary by location, so expect adaptation for alignment with your local context and legal requirements. Reflection questions at the end of each chapter and related worksheets provide application exercises to use individually or in a group study with finance or stewardship teams or others interested in strengthening church ministry. The appendices offer additional resources and policy samples. I am honored to share this journey with you whether you are excited, anxious, or just curious. Strengthening your financial leadership will bless your mission efforts and bring you joy!

Receive this blessing: Well begun, good and faithful steward.

Reflection Questions

1. Describe the missional purpose of your church. What does your faith community value?
2. What does it mean to be part of God's mission in the world?
3. Share an example that describes your personal or corporate attitude about money.
4. Share an example of generosity.
5. If Jesus chaired your financial ministry or headed up your stewardship campaign, what would be different?
6. What messages have you heard from your church leaders, friends, or family about the relationship between faith and finances?
7. Could your finances be reframed as mission resources? If so, how will you begin?

CHAPTER ONE

BIBLICAL WISDOM FOR FINANCIAL MANAGEMENT FOR MISSION

How can we not be giddy with gratitude
and reckless generosity
for all the gifts God has given us?

—Steve Garnaas-Holmes

Our mission to share Christ's love, hope, and healing thrives when we are aligned with scripture, grounded in our Wesleyan spirituality, and connected to our membership vows of prayer, presence, gifts, service, and witness. The following biblical tenets embody these values and connect our biblical understanding of God's generosity with our call to serve others. These plumb lines for stewardship offer a Wesleyan compass for financial decision making and management of resources. They speak to how our foundational beliefs shape our worldview and influence our life choices and stewardship behaviors. Even if they sound familiar, each represents a vital spiritual discipline deserving periodic reexamination for our personal lives and the missions we lead.

Everything Is a Gift from God

> The people rejoiced . . . for they had given freely and wholeheartedly to the LORD. David the king also rejoiced greatly.
>
> David praised the LORD in the presence of the whole assembly, saying,
>
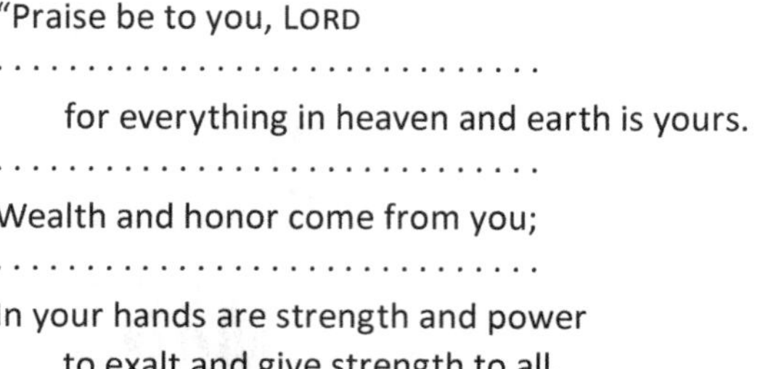

> "Praise be to you, LORD
> . . . .
> for everything in heaven and earth is yours.
> . . . .
> Wealth and honor come from you;
> . . . .
> In your hands are strength and power
> to exalt and give strength to all.
> Now, our God, we give you thanks,
> and praise your glorious name." (1 Chr. 29:9-13)

We acknowledge God's abundant generosity and creativity during prayer, hopefully even during daily living! Like King David celebrating the gifts provided to build the temple, approaching life from this perspective causes us to radiate joy and grace. Speak the words "everything is a gift from God" out loud and observe how your body responds. I am smiling; are you?

This first biblical touchstone summons us to live gratefully, the first step in a lifetime of discipleship. Appreciation for God's abundant creation inspires generous acts of gratitude. Research on healing and giving confirms the positive impact of generosity and the power of affirmation and gratitude, regardless of one's situation. Whether blessed with a charmed life or living with chronic illness, there are abundant testimonials correlating acts of generosity and gratitude with positive benefits.

Prayer Pause: Give thanks to God for the greatest gift you ever received. Acknowledge the greatest challenge and God's presence in that time. Note how giving thanks feels physically and emotionally.

Gratitude reframes our economic position from owners to stewards, from givers to receivers, from collectors to distributors. Our values shift from security to sufficiency. Even while proclaiming this belief, cultural messages urge us to collect and hoard. Spiritually, we know we are free only when willing to give everything away, because we never really own anything. Imagine your mission living fully committed to acknowledging God's ownership of everything.

We Are Chosen by God

> You did not choose me, but I chose you and appointed you so that you might go and bear fruit—fruit that will last—and so that whatever you ask in my name the Father will give you. (John 15:16)

We are stewards by design, made in God's image, endowed with gifts, and expected to bear fruit. Like modern-day trustees, our *chosen* status invokes both honor and responsibility. Discovering we are chosen is another gift we learn to receive.

Prayer Pause: What is God's purpose for you? For your church?

If you aren't sure you are chosen, loved, and accepted by God, read Acts 8:26-40. An angel sends Phillip to an Ethiopian eunuch, whose questions about Isaiah's texts lead to his baptism by Phillip. Surely this story is preserved as assurance that God accepts all, even strangers, even those tortured or cast aside by society.

Dennise chose me while homeless and welcomed me into her family's life and challenges. After taking her family to the New England Aquarium, I treated them to lunch. Leaving the diner, we saw a woman holding a "Please help" sign. Dennise reached into her pocket, drew out some coins and dropped them in the woman's cup. Dennise then told her children, "There is always someone whose needs are greater than ours." Dennise's act of generosity, given from her limited resources, taught me that God equips everyone to be both a giver and receiver.

As chosen children of God, equipped with power and love, we are responsible for the well-being of all of creation, including its people. In our relationships with one another, do we build up others or tear them down? Do we care for others as we care for ourselves? Do we know when to protect what has been built or let it all go for God? Stewards face questions without easy answers! These responsibilities require courage and discipline. As

God's trustworthy stewards, we are accountable to God and one another. Financial management and stewardship practices strengthen our commitment to God's vision. Therefore, we must deeply consider our relationship with money and the allure of consumerism, and raise questions about sustainability and the impact of our daily choices on God's creation. We steward God's mission through wise stewardship, compassionate love, and powerful self-discipline. Are we ready?

God Has a Preference for the Poor

> Suppose a brother or sister is without clothes and daily food. If one of you says to them, "Go in peace; keep warm and well fed," but does nothing about their physical needs, what good is it? In the same way, faith by itself, if it is not accompanied by action, is dead. (Jas. 2:15-17)

The mission priorities of stewards emulate God's preference for the poor. God's priorities come first, before our interests. Trustees and other financial managers have the fiduciary responsibility to act in the best interest of the owner. As extensions of Jesus's ministry, we serve all persons, including the afflicted and poor. We may experience poverty in spirit, health, generosity, or wealth ourselves, but because we know the abundance and generosity of God's creation, we can believe that God provides sufficient resources for the world. They may, however, need to be redistributed. Our faithful stewardship, acts of generosity, and participation in justice honor God's priorities every time missional acts impact the lives of others.

Prayer Pause: Identify the mission projects your faith community supports. Which mission projects do you personally support? Do we understand all our mission activity as sacred expressions of God's love?

A steward continually honors God's wishes. Our faithful mission is greater than a response to social needs; many groups practice acts of mercy and justice. Rather, we are chosen to steward and share the gifts with which God has blessed us so others may know the love of God through us. Clarity about our mission focus strengthens our stewardship activities and inspires generosity. In God's economy, the phrase "money follows mission" bears true, especially when our mission aligns with God's priorities. People support authentic mission work, giving even more when they know the effect of their gifts. In my own experience, when church members learned I was driving homeless families to doctor's appointments and church, they pressed money into my hands. The desire to participate in God's mission is irresistible. When we steward God's mission, generosity multiplies gifts. Trusting this truth is a spiritual discipline.

When Dennise's son Joan joined the Job Corp, we visited a local department store to prepare him for the cold Maine winter. Estimating the cost to keep him safe and warm at about $100, I soon realized that boots, gloves, a coat, and the desired hat and long underwear would stretch my generosity. Choosing to trust God's plan, I somewhat begrudgingly paid for his supplies, only to be blessed two days later with an unanticipated stipend for the same amount we spent in the department store. Trust and obey! Discover the joy and freedom of trusting God's plan.

Today Matters

> Love does no harm to a neighbor. Therefore love is the fulfillment of the law.
>
> And do this, understanding the present time: The hour has already come for you to wake up from your slumber, because our salvation is nearer now than when we first believed. (Rom. 13:10-11)

The simplest disciplines are often the hardest to practice. Whether seeking to improve our physical fitness or financial health, the undeniable truth is that every decision affects our future options. Since every day is a gift, each day we postpone a task or choice, we alter our future possibilities. For example, when people start early to establish saving habits and continue to practice this through their lives, they create future options, especially with compounding interest. How I wish I had practiced the discipline recommended by the local bank when they gave our second-grade class passbook savings accounts to watch our pennies grow. Procrastinating planning and action usually limits future choices. Since we don't know what tomorrow will bring, today matters.

"Do today what should not be put off until tomorrow" is a saying with significant meaning and consequences. Online debt and savings calculators help us see how the choices we make to save, spend, or borrow affect our future. When a loved one dies with unclear estate planning or without a *will*, the pain and distress of this difficult time increases. When financial stewardship disciplines, such as budgeting, are left to another day, some opportunities are lost forever. Our worries about money and persistent avoidance of financial stewardship must change. Otherwise, we risk never experiencing the well-being and enjoyment of creation God desires for us.

Prayer Pause: What stewardship or financial decisions have you avoided? What is your faith community or mission avoiding? What is sustaining that avoidance? Do you see new possibilities for your life and your mission? What is your first step? Take it.

A variety of personal and cultural dynamics influence our *dis*-ease in talking about money and financial stewardship. What is true in our personal lives is typically also true in our professional lives. Jesus spoke about money and financial choices consistently and clearly. His countercultural invitation to the disciples was honest transparency about giving, missions, generosity, the balance of power, and the distribution of resources among peoples. Practicing informed planning and decision making is faithful stewardship.

The four biblical, financial-stewardship perspectives shared in this chapter do not guarantee safety and security, but they can inform our mission activities and responsibilities as stewards, clarifying our role in God's creation and reminding us of God's generosity. A faithful steward practices generosity today and every day. See **Worksheet 1** for personal or group exploration of biblical stewardship. Grounded in this biblical wisdom, we are ready to tackle practical financial stewardship skills.

Reflection Questions

1. How do the four principles covered in this chapter clarify, align with, or expand your definition of stewardship?

2. Who is a generous person you know? A mission-focused person? Are these the kinds of people leading your mission efforts?
3. What scripture comes to mind when you think about money? About your church finances?
4. Which principle would you like to strengthen in your life or profession?
5. What are your greatest challenges regarding money and financial stewardship, personally and professionally?
6. Name two ways these four principles impact your life or profession. Share two ways to begin living according to these beliefs.
7. What is your favorite biblical teaching about money? Why?

CHAPTER TWO

FINANCIAL VOCABULARY

What's in a word?
Anything and everything.

Stewards of money for mission encounter many financial terms, some with multiple meanings. Some words are synonyms used randomly in financial communications. Some have legal as well financial definitions. Familiarity with these key concepts provides a solid foundation for financial stewardship leadership, and it will help you talk intelligently to finance professionals. You will find additional information about many of these terms in other chapters. Browse through this language lexicon at your leisure or as needed.

Vocabulary List

Account

When used as a noun, *account* identifies a category of money or a location where money is placed. *Account* also identifies specific funds such as Blessed Missions Savings Account, or a specific use, for example, Vacation Bible School Account. Because of multiple usages, including as a verb, precise descriptive titles provide important clarification. Also see *Fund*.

Asset

A resource a person or organization owns or stewards is an *asset.* Examples include a building, an endowment fund, or a valuable item such as a high-quality piano. Assets may have insurance coverage to protect them from damage or loss. Liquid *assets* are cash or resources easily converted to cash without loss of value, for example, funds in a bank account. Non-liquid assets, such as property, are harder to sell and their value may fluctuate. Full disclosure of assets is required of nonprofit organizations.

Audit

This is an inventory of all assets stewarded by an organization and an assessment of practices and policies guiding financial processes and reports. The purpose of an audit is to assess the accuracy of financial information and whether reports offer a complete and fair representation of the financial position. Audits also reduce risk to the persons involved in money management because all funds, accounts, investments and property are inventoried. Churches with budgets under $500,000 typically conduct an audit review rather than a more expensive professional audit. Reviewing account balances and financial procedures annually promotes best practices that safeguard resources and communicate accurately.

Balance Sheet

Providing a summary of assets and financial obligations, the *balance sheet* is a financial report summarizing the financial position of an organization. When the report includes all assets, such as property and debts, leaders see the complete financial reality when planning and making decisions. Financial reports typically focus on the annual budget. The balance sheet offers a broader summary by including fixed assets, such as property and high-cost equipment (e.g., vehicles), as well as current and long-term debt, and arrearages (payments due to others). Balance sheets explain, for example, whether loan payments of $10,000 in an annual budget are applied to a loan balance of $50,000 or $500,000, and the actual value of an endowment or investments generating income for the annual budget. Knowing whether an asset's value is $1,000 or $1,000,000 impacts overall financial well-being. Too often, finance leaders make decisions without a balance sheet report that provides this type of clarifying information.

Budget

Typically adopted one year at a time, a *budget* is a system for tracking financial transactions during a period of time. Budgets help leaders plan and manage the mission's financial position by setting goals for *income* and *expenses.* Budgets are typically presented as a series of numbers recording income (money received or available to support the mission) and *expenses* (money paid out for costs related to the mission work). The *balance* or bottom line is the difference between the amount of income received and the expenses to be paid. In a budget report, a positive balance means more income than expenses at that time; a negative balance indicates expenses are greater than income. A balanced budget indicates income equal to expenses, or within a range of acceptable variance, say, less than 3 to 5 percent. Budgets monitor financial transactions; however, many other factors affect financial health and stability. The impact of these factors may show up quickly or slowly in budget reports.

Campaign

A generic term for a process for requesting financial support, *campaigns* may focus on specific types of projects or financial needs. An annual support campaign for the operations budget is managed differently from a capital campaign, where external support such as a consultant affects results. Campaigns may include pledges or commitment forms, have short-term or long-term goals, and may be implemented in person, or by mail, email, phone, or social media. Annual commitment requests, often called stewardship campaigns, inviting promises of financial support for the next budget period, correlate highly with effective financial stewardship and are strongly recommended. Previous experiences and the military connotations of the word *campaign* create opportunities to develop alternative language and invitation models. Numerous resources on campaign models exist with varying commitments of time and resources.

Cash Flow

Income and expenses vary greatly during a budget period, creating times when expenses are greater than the funds available in the bank account. *Cash flow* needs will fluctuate as income and expenses occur during the budget period. Managing cash flow ensures funds cover expenses so that bank account balances remain positive. Cash-flow reserve funds are used when needed for expenses that exceed the current budget's income. Replenishing cash-flow reserves occurs when resources become available. Cash-flow management contributes to financial health and stability.

Endowment

An *endowment* is a permanently protected fund, created to generate future income. The original gift, also known as principle or corpus, is not used unless permission is given in a policy or in bequest language. Generally, only the earnings or income are available for use and may be distributed or reinvested. Endowed funds are often invested, as they will exist for a long period of time. Governing policies or bequest language in a *will* describing the gift determines whether any interest or dividends from investments in bonds or stocks/equities are distributed. Bequests also set any expectations regarding the purpose of the funds. Good documentation and recordkeeping are important because these long-term funds will be stewarded by others in the future.

Expenses

The costs of fulfilling our mission are *expenses*. Some expenses are due immediately; others are payable within a designated period of time, typically thirty days. Expenses are an obligation or commitment by the organization. When expenses are deferred beyond their due date, they become arrearages. Unpaid expenses or accounts payable are reported on a balance sheet and should be included in a monthly financial report. Financial reports should also include the full amount of connectional commitments or apportionments due and donated services such as a volunteer organist, to provide clarity about total expenses. In budget reports, expenses are compared to income to monitor cash flow and budget health.

Fiduciary Responsibility

This is a commitment and obligation to choose actions in the best interests of another person or organization, which has entrusted resources in your care. A *fiduciary* prioritizes the asset owner's needs over personal interests or preferences. Laws govern who acts as a fiduciary, and a fiduciary relationship has legal consequences when actions taken are not in the best interest of the owner. As administrative officers,[1] pastors need to understand fiduciary expectations. Similarly, as stewards of God's creation, God's vision is more important than our own.

Fund

As a noun, *fund* describes a category of money, or a place money is held, or a way money will be used. Careful use is recommended because *fund* may also represent multiple aspects of an accounting and financial management system. For example, *fund* may represent a specific bank account, or a sub-account within a financial recordkeeping system, or the title of resources for a project or activity, such as a Memorial Fund. Or, *fund* may identify specific uses of money, such as Adult Education Funds. Clear descriptive use will convey your financial system's structure and mission activities. Donor trust, confidence, and generosity improve when our financial systems are easy to understand.

Funds may also be identified as *designated* or *restricted.* Organizations create designations that may be added or removed based on current needs. Donors create restrictions that may or may not be acceptable to the receiving organization. For more information, see chapter 5.

Generosity

Synonyms for *generosity* include acts of kindness, openheartedness, and bounty. Also synonymous with charity and a belief that, with God, anything is possible, one recommendation for financial challenges is to create a culture of generosity. Trusting God and joyfully giving more of what we have received grows our faith.

Generosity is the sacred and miraculous ingredient that opens hearts and wallets for the good of others. Generosity inspires people to share joyfully, and to give more than they previously believed possible, and it challenges consumerism by supporting mission alternatives like Advent Conspiracy.[2] With twenty-four hours' notice, my church generously donated twenty-four

---

1 "Responsibilities and Duties of Elders and Licensed Pastors," in *The Book of Discipline of The United Methodist Church: 2016* (Nashville, TN: The United Methodist Publishing House, 2016), ¶340.2.c (2); "The Charge Conference," in *The Discipline*, ¶244.3.

2 www.adventconspiracy.org.

suitcases for homeless families living in a local hotel. Sometimes still difficult to define, we recognize generosity when we see it.

> "Bring the whole tithe into the storehouse, that there may be food in my house. Test me in this," says the LORD Almighty, "and see if I will not throw open the floodgates of heaven and pour out so much blessing that there will not be room enough to store it." (Mal. 3:10)

Despite the clear invitational challenge in Malachi 3:10, faithful generosity doesn't expect a response from God. However, many times the blessings experienced when we give generously match or exceed the cost of the gift given. Spiritual giant Henri Nouwen offers his experience of surprise income equal to the amount he gave a young traveler for a train ticket home.[3] Have you experienced being tested or testing God and discovering unexpected blessings? Have you noticed how often the decision to give an extraordinary gift of money, time, or resources is quickly followed by the receipt of a surprise gift yourself? If you have, tell your generosity story to a friend.

Gift

An object given freely and without expectations is a *gift*, also representing a transfer of ownership from one party to another. Gifts include money, tangible goods, property, or investments such as stocks—also called equities—or bonds. Some gifts require approval by the recipient and may be refused. Often, the giver has an expectation of a benefit to the recipient. The giver also typically experiences a positive emotional and psychological response. After a gift is completed, the donor relinquishes control or influence over the gift and may not add or revise restrictions or give direction for the use of the funds. Please reread the last sentence! Strong relationships between donors and missions make this boundary setting complicated. The purpose of this boundary is to protect the donor from any real or perceived conflicts of interest.

Gifts trigger emotional, spiritual, and sometimes economic benefits for

---

3 Henri J. M. Nouwen, *A Spirituality of Fundraising* (Nashville, TN: Upper Room Books, 2010), v.

donors. When gifts are accepted and acknowledged by nonprofit organizations, donors are sometimes eligible for tax benefits. When the giver receives a tangible benefit such as dinner or concert tickets, part of their gift is a transaction. Tax laws and charitable giving regulations may place additional limits on certain gifts. Check with a local advisor or attorney, especially for large gifts.

Gratitude

The act of expressing thanks or appreciation is *gratitude*. How often should we say thank you for gifts of time, talent, and money for mission? We seldom offer enough gratitude and almost always offer too little. Leadership improves morale, self-esteem, and generosity by multiplying the ways gratitude is expressed. For example, during an offertory invitation, I casually said, "Thank you for all you have already done" for an international mission project. The congregation spontaneously took another offering for the same project the next week. Just eight words of gratitude inspired them to give more for mission.

Each gift is an invitation to say thank you. Each thank you is an invitation to give again. One is not complete without the other. This least expensive financial stewardship activity is frequently underutilized. The simplest form of gratitude, saying thank you more often, is a great first step for increasing funding for missions.

Income

Resources that *come in* and are available for use for ministry expenses are *income*, also known as revenue. Income is often cash, checks, or electronic transfers given by members. Other income is generated by activities and events, some of which are fundraisers. Some items, such as stocks or property, are converted to cash to generate income. Recurring income, such as weekly offerings, are ongoing and reliable, and while windfalls, such as bequests or the sale of assets, may be larger, they are less reliable.

Generating income equal to or greater than expenses increases financial stability. Expanding income is often perceived as difficult; however, it is much healthier than reducing vital expenses in most situations. Focusing on giving donors opportunities to make life-giving gifts is more effective than emphasizing the mission's need to receive funding. Increasing income grows missions; increased missions grows income.

Investment

In financial settings, *investment* identifies resources placed at a financial institution that purchases and trades stocks or bonds. In the long run, investments typically generate significantly more income than bank accounts; however, investments are subject to market fluctuations and not protected by FDIC coverage like many bank accounts. Risk tolerance and the time-horizon for the asset affect the type of investments to consider. Endowments are often invested.

Liability

Debts such as loans and unpaid bills or accounts payable are *liabilities*. They are commitments made previously for future payments, often over multiple budget periods. People and organizations have different feelings about liabilities. Taking on debt may be strategic, for example, to complete a construction project during good weather, when pledges supporting the project continue into the next year. Some people find passing on debts to future generations unacceptable. Also described as "robbing Peter to pay Paul," the practice of borrowing from one asset or fund to cover another expense is discouraged. For multiple reasons, long-term *liabilities* are risky business for missional entities.

Profit

Technically, *profit* identifies a positive fund balance when expenses are deducted from income. Nonprofit organizations are expected to reinvest income exceeding expenses back into the mission. While not to be confused with *prophecy*, how profits are reinvested communicates a message donors and communities may hear more clearly than the biblical prophets.

Profit and Loss Statement (P&L)

A summary financial report of assets and liabilities during a specific period of time is called a *P&L statement*. Financial reports should include all sources of income and all liabilities due or in arrears during the budget time period. A comprehensive monthly or quarterly financial report serves as the profit and loss statement, also known as a financial report. Supplementing this periodic report with current bank account balances provides a more complete financial status report.

Stewardship

Stewardship, often reduced to a fall fundraising appeal, is more accurately a way of life that demonstrates our Christian discipleship to the world. As disciples, we seek to live the way Jesus invited us to live. Wayne Barrett defined *stewardship* as "the name we give to the practical expression of our faith."[4] Since money makes our missions possible, stewardship includes, but is not limited to, managing and raising funds for missions. Waiting for financial security before stepping out in mission sounds fiscally responsible; however, growth-oriented leaders recognize that mission activity motivates giving. Mission activity is not always risk-free, and risk aversion impedes mission capacity, creating stewardship dilemmas. Risk-averse financial leaders and risk-tolerant visionaries prioritize different aspects of stewardship. Because donors seek increasing transparency about how their gifts are used and who is impacted by their generosity, mission is the central generosity-cultivating activity. In addition to financial knowledge, stewardship requires courage, leadership, vision, and risk tolerance as our missions respond to the world's needs.

FOUNDATIONAL STATEMENT ON STEWARDSHIP AND GENEROSITY

Stewardship is whatever we do with what God has entrusted to us by the way that we live. In response to God's outpouring love and covenant faithfulness, we live out of God's abundance instead of the illusion of scarcity thinking. We seek to nurture generous living in ourselves and others, affirming the redemptive power of the gospel of Jesus Christ and expressing our confidence in God's transforming work among us.

This beautiful natural world is a loving gift from God. Together we pledge ourselves to assist God's vision of creation's renewal, to advocate for justice and peace, to measure our carbon footprint, and to practice hope

4 Wayne Barrett, *Get Well, Stay Well: Prescriptions for a Financially Healthy Congregation* (Nashville, TN: Discipleship Resources, 1998), 3.

as we support transforming ministries, becoming better stewards of God's creation.

Trusting in the presence of the Risen Christ and of the Holy Spirit among us, we embrace the spiritual discipline of first fruits living: offering to God the first and the best of all God has given us and managing all the rest according to God's generosity. This daily practice includes giving our prayers, presence, gifts, service, and witness on God's behalf.[5]

Tithe

Traditionally one-tenth portion, we understand a *tithe* as a goal for faithful giving to God's mission. Biblical texts describe multiple tithes; current discussions about tithing debate whether a tithe is based on before-tax or after-tax income. The stewardship discipline of setting a goal to give joyfully from our first fruits to God blesses donors. Challenging and inviting tithing goes in and out of vogue with different generations; those who tithe consistently testify that it works.

Trustee

In legal terminology, a *trustee* manages others' resources according to the owner's instructions and with the owner's best interests in mind. Persons or organizations, such as a bank or foundation, may serve as trustees. Leaders elected as trustees typically manage property and certain assets. Church trustees are accountable to the governing body—the Church Council and the Charge Conference—and are not independent entities. Trustees may manage specific accounts or investments on behalf of the mission's goals. Trustees are highly accountable and are called to be trustworthy stewards.

Reflection Questions

1. Imagine Jesus describing your finances. What words would he add to those covered in this chapter?

---

5 https://www.umcdiscipleship.org/resources/foundation-statement-on-stewardship-and-generosity. Adapted from UM Council of Bishops' Pastoral Letter in *God's Renewed Creation: Call to Hope and Action* (2009).

2. Are any of these words still unclear in your mind? Where can you find additional definitions?
3. Share some other terms that impact our understanding of financial stewardship.
4. How have you seen words and their meanings confuse or undermine missions? How have you seen words strengthen mission?
5. How do these terms clarify or complexify your understanding of the relationship between finances and stewardship?
6. Which of these terms and definitions apply to you?

CHAPTER THREE

MANAGING GOD'S MONEY

Personal Financial Stewardship

You could, if your heart were open,
be startled into giving away your estate
at the sight of a single red berry in autumn,
and never know poverty.

—Steve Garnaas-Holmes

Our personal financial health and our professional well-being and effectiveness are interrelated and interdependent, as a growing body of research confirms. Growth in our personal financial stewardship disciplines positively influences our leadership effectiveness and the missions we support. Our spiritual journey integrates a deeper relationship with God with attentive listening to the world's missional needs, both of which are impacted by our relationship with money. Explore this phase of your leadership journey in this chapter and in related worksheets. Be courageous. Personal stewardship reminds us to remove the log from our own eye before assisting others (Matt. 7:1-5; Luke 6:42). Jesus described it as being as hard as going through the eye of a needle (Mark 10:25; Matt. 19:24).

Beginning Again: An Invitation for All Stewards

Stewardship is a lifelong endeavor that influences the choices we make during our lives, and it includes more than money. We discover the gifts God invites us to steward: gifts of leadership, vision, compassion, healing, exhortation, *and* money. Throughout our lives, we develop a relationship with money that too often impairs us rather than empowering our joyful stewardship. Some of us keep meticulous records about our finances; others choose not to worry as long as the bank account balance is positive. When we don't have our financial house in order, our spiritual and temporal life is vulnerable. Expecting bank or asset/investment managers to steward our bank accounts with our best interests in mind assumes they know our values and goals. When one family member handles the financial responsibilities and decisions while the others trust blindly, a crisis can lead to chaos. God's stewards are called to greater discipline and accountability, especially with money, because, as Jesus recognized, we too easily want to put money above God. Money becomes our god, and that is idolatry.

Yet our faith promises a new beginning each day, a chance to create or reestablish spiritual disciplines and stewardship practices. Whether beginning or resuming this journey, clarify where you are before looking toward a desired destination. Your goals—avoiding or reducing debt or increasing savings for education or retirement—will depend on your current situation. If you know nothing about your financial situation, begin the spiritual discipline of stewarding your life today. If you consider yourself well informed about your financial situation, remember that your will or estate plan, if it exists, should be reviewed and updated annually. As you review or engage in personal financial stewardship, consider this question: Am I being as generous with the resources I steward as God has been with me? Since sufficiency and generosity go hand in hand, address the fears constraining your generosity. They may also be impairing your financial stability.

As you explore the reflection questions in **Worksheet 2: Personal Stewardship**, listen to your heart. **Worksheets 3–5** explore stewardship in your personal life and faith journey. There are no wrong answers, only opportunities to grow deeper in our understanding and practice of the spiritual disciplines of stewarding money. As a leader, others will not follow where we are not willing to go, so our courage and integrity as financial stewards affects our lives and the lives of all who look to us as leaders for inspiration, guidance, and direction. After your personal experience with these worksheets, consider sharing them in a group setting. Our mission endeavors and professional ministry careers now require us to be financially literate. Some of us will need to move outside our comfort zones to lead our mission endeavors. Whether you use these tools individually, in a group setting, or even with a coach, this exploration will deepen and renew your faith and trust in God's abundant love for each of us: God's stewards.

Discovering Gifts

Disciple-making leadership asks others to share their personal visions and professional gifts so that missional activities steward those resources for the greatest impact. Some gifts may fit your mission; some may better align with others' visions. Some visions are seeds that require planting multiple times.

Successfully linking gifts and talents to opportunities for changing the world and meeting human need is another aspect of stewardship. Before asking others, we also need to consider our own gifts and call. A variety of gift inventories or spiritual gifts tools are available online or from denominational resources including this example: http://www.umc.org/what-we-believe/spiritual-gifts-online-assessment.[1] Spiritual-gifts inventories increase our knowledge about others and ourselves, contributing positively to our stewardship endeavors. Discovering gifts will strengthen your stewardship of talents, deepen relationships, and increase your joy and alignment of gifts with commitments.

When we successfully align people's calls with the world's needs, empathy and generosity connect personal motivation and resource commitments, including money. Hence, generosity and money flow from our stewardship of people's passions and visions for mission. Use **Worksheet 6: Discover Your Gifts Inventory** to clarify your personal motivations and gifts, and then ask

---

1 This online gifts assessment is based on the book *Equipped for Every Good Work* by Barbara Dick and Dan R. Dick (Eugene, OR: Wipf and Stock, 2011). See also its companion website, http://equippedforeverygoodwork.wordpress.com, for further details and tools. Another example: http://www.umc.org/what-we-believe/spiritual-gifts-online-assessment.

other leaders these questions as a stewardship of gifts exercise. Celebrate the discovery.

About Financial Gifts

We want our gifts to change the world. Explore the giving strategies described in the following sections that are appropriate for your situation. Some information about financial investments and giving options currently available online disguise sales pitches as information, while denominational resources and development officers are committed to the church's and your best interests.[2]

Many of us simply don't know our potential. Your best gift to the next generation may be urging them to save for retirement even while paying off other debts, equipping them for greater security and generosity in the future. Our greatest opportunity to be generous may be using assets to create a legacy through a planned gift. Regardless of the size of your assets, being generous will multiply God's gifts. Contact your annual conference's Foundation for educational resources about the impact of future gifts through stewardship planning today. Find a guide or a buddy to explore with you. As we talk more honestly about personal finances, we create a culture of confidence and competence with financial responsibilities and opportunities, develop skills and stewardship knowledge, and share the joy of generosity. As airplane stewards regularly remind passengers, place the oxygen mask on your own face first before assisting others. These are also wise words for pastoral leaders insecure about financial matters and ready to grow as stewardship leaders.

Gifts also create a relationship between the giver and those benefiting from their generosity. Maimonides, a twelfth-century Jewish scholar, created a ladder of gift characteristics, each step toward the top representing different giving styles. Consider this list and its implications for our giving attitudes and expectations about generosity.

---

2 Books such as Adam Hamilton, *Enough: Discovering Joy through Simplicity and Generosity* (Nashville, TN: Abingdon Press, 2012) offer faith-based wisdom for personal finances, cultural challenges, and practical ways to live with biblical financial stewardship principles.

MAIMONIDES'S LADDER[3]

Highest Value

1. Giving money, a loan, your time, or a partnership that benefits the recipient and prevents them from becoming dependent on others
2. Giving anonymously to unknown recipient
3. Giving anonymously when you know the recipient
4. Giving to anonymous recipient with your name attached to the gift
5. Giving before being asked
6. Giving when asked
7. Giving less than appropriate amounts, but pleasantly
8. Giving begrudgingly or sorrowfully

Lowest Value

Kinds of Financial Gifts

People support the missions they cherish in many ways, and some giving options offer additional benefits for donors. Some financial gifts described below don't require financial or legal counsel. Some have estate and tax consequences; be aware that legal counsel is recommended for all significant gifts. Gifts of property or assets, such as stocks or valuable items, as well as income-generating gifts, such as gift annuities or charitable trusts, require consultation with professional advisors.

Appreciated Assets

When held for a long period of time, some assets, such as savings bonds, property, or stocks, can grow in value. In some cases, the tax incurred when selling appreciated assets causes owners to hold these resources longer than they need or wish. By gifting appreciated assets to a nonprofit mission, they are sold and converted to cash without tax implications. Selling

---

3 Adapted from https://www.jewishvirtuallibrary.org/eight-levels-of-charitable-giving, citing as source Haym Donin, *To Be a Jew: A Guide to Jewish Observance in Contemporary Life* (New York: Basic Books, 1991).

and investing appreciated assets is safer for churches and nonprofits than holding stock or bond certificates, which are too easily misplaced. Your local United Methodist Foundation may help convert appreciated assets, including stocks, into a charitable gift of cash. Valuable items, such as jewelry or precious metals or collectibles, may also be gifted to some charities. Resources to support your vision as a partner in God's work may exist in your home or safety deposit box.

Beneficiary Designations

Financial assets, such as insurance policies, individual retirement accounts, pension funds, and other investments, include opportunities to identify a beneficiary. Individuals may list people or nonprofits, such as churches or mission sites, as beneficiaries for all or a percentage of an asset when they die. Beneficiary designations are stewarded by the asset manager—bank or financial institution—placing the distribution-process responsibility in their hands. Using a beneficiary designation to gift assets can avoid the probate court process and distribute your gifts more quickly. Because beneficiary designations may be changed during your lifetime, they create a flexible option for creative generosity.

Cash Gifts

Donors regularly make gifts with cash or through pledges paid over a specific period of time. Cash is the simplest form of gift, and donors should always consult their financial advisor before making significant gifts of cash. Alternatives to cash gifts could be more appropriate options for certain donors. Churches may wish to encourage large donors to explore other options to maximize the stewardship of their resources. For tax purposes, cash donations require written gift acknowledgments, also known as gift substantiation, and include the phrase "no gifts or services received in exchange for this gift."[4] A surprise gift, also known as a *windfall* gift, from an estate or winnings, can cause joy or harm to the church and donor depending on the stewardship disciplines practiced.

---

4 Department of the Treasury Internal Revenue Service, *Charitable Contributions: Substantiation and Disclosure Requirements*, IRS Exempt Organizations, (Publication 1771 [Rev. 3-2016], Catalog Number 20054Q), https://www.irs.gov/pub/irs-pdf/p1771.pdf.

Charitable Gift Annuity/Trusts

Some donors may choose gift options that provide income for life and then distribute gifts to a nonprofit at the end of their lives. These gifts offer investment earnings well above market value. For example, 8.7 percent for eighty-seven-year-old donors creating charitable gift annuities[5] may reduce some taxes and will distribute income to the donor and then to the donor's chosen nonprofits at the time of death.

A charitable gift annuity is a permanent gift managed by a gift annuity provider who invests the funds and then distributes income to the donors during their lifetimes. The income distributed to the donors is determined by the donor's age at the time of the gift, so older donors receive higher returns. A partial charitable tax deduction occurs the year the gift is made because the donor receives payments for life. Yearly distributions to the donor are partially tax-free, eventually becoming taxable as the donor ages. Charitable gift annuity sponsors may require a $1,000 to $5,000 minimum, and these life-income gifts may be much larger. Other life-income gifts include a variety of charitable trusts for gifts, usually exceeding $100,000. Trust agreements range from percentage-based distributions to specific distribution amounts to deferred, or time-designated, distributions. These options create flexibility to meet donors' personal situations and goals. Always consult a planned giving professional and personal tax or estate advisors when considering a charitable gift annuity or trust agreement. Your local United Methodist Foundation may offer charitable gift annuities and trust management for gifts to benefit a variety of missions.

Endowments: Creating an Annual Pledge or Family Endowment

When a gift creates an endowment, it generates financial support forever. Yes, forever! Endowed gifts of $500 or $1,000 in the last century have grown to thousands of protected dollars now, blessing current missions with steady financial support. The source of an endowed gift could be cash, stocks, a life insurance policy, property, or a gift annuity. An endowed gift created

---

5 Rate recommendations provided by American Council on Gift Annuities. Current report located at https://www.acga-web.org/gift-annuity-rates. See Single Life–ACGA Suggested Gift Annuity Rates Table, updated June 15, 2018.

during your lifetime or through your estate plan provides income to the missions you support during your lifetime and beyond. Curious how this works?

Endowment status protects the principal of a gift, which is typically invested for greater potential for financial growth. The beneficiary organization or mission named by the donor receives income from the investment based on the investment performance and distribution policies adopted for the endowment. Distributions may be deferred, allowing the funds to grow for a period of time or set at a certain percentage rate or dollar amount.

In the following example, we will assume the investment performance of a gift generates a 5 percent average rate of return. Donors may allow a gift to grow for a period of time—deferring distributions—which accelerates the fund's potential growth. This chart demonstrates the possible growth of invested gifts, the power of compounding interest and market growth.

ANNUAL INCOME POTENTIAL OF ENDOWED GIFTS*

A gift of	May provide annual income of
$2,000	$100
$5,000	$250
$10,000	$500
$20,000	$1,000
$50,000	$2,500
$100,000	$5,000

*In about twenty years, with no distributions, a 5 percent return annually could double the size of the original gift. Annual distributions slow down growth, but eventually the distributions could exceed the original gift and continue to increase. Long-term planning will have the most impact.

Check with your local United Methodist Foundation or denominational foundations to explore options for creating a donor-designated fund or family endowment to benefit your favorite mission.

Required Minimum Distributions

Be aware that current tax laws require persons over the age of seventy and a half to draw a portion of their retirement plan funds annually. These required minimum distributions (RMD) may push some donors up into higher tax brackets. Tax laws now allow donors to transfer their required minimum distribution from most retirement funds directly to a nonprofit and avoid receiving the distribution as taxable income. The distribution must be sent directly to the nonprofit by the fund administrator. Contact your retirement plan manager to request this distribution option and confirm current tax regulations and options.[6]

Totten Trust or "Pay on Death Account"

Individuals may open a bank account or certificate of deposit that identifies a nonprofit as the beneficiary. The remaining balance in the account is distributed upon death notification. This gift is completed without legal counsel and doesn't go through probate; however, the funds may be required to cover the donor's personal debt before distribution to the beneficiary. A Totten Trust or "Pay On Death" (POD) account is accessible by the donor during his or her lifetime. The beneficiary has no access to the funds during the donor's lifetime. Regardless of your estate size, this is a simple way to begin building your legacy.

Wills and Bequests

A *Will* (capitalized in this chapter for clarity) is a legal document describing your wishes for your assets and care of minor children following your death. Without a Will, you are *intestate* and your estate is stewarded by the state government. In addition to charging fees and not knowing your wishes, this process may not benefit your heirs and will not benefit any of your favorite missions. Complete an estate inventory to discover the full value of your accumulated resources, which is probably more than you realize. Describing your wishes through a Will documents your preferences and may simplify settling your estate—going through probate—which will involve legal counsel and costs. If you wish to support any mission beyond your lifetime, record that information in your Will. The following examples illustrate some

---

6 See https://www.irs.gov/retirement-plans/plan-participant-employee/retirement-topics-required-minimum-distributions-rmds. Sections on required minimum distributions and qualified charitable distributions. Also see Pub. 590-B, Distributions from Individual Retirement Arrangements (IRAs). Some United Methodist pension funds may not be eligible.

distributions or gift designations options. Remember to always seek local legal counsel for your estate plan.

- To calculate a gift either before or after other gifts are distributed: *I give this gift [before or after] the distributions I have documented for my estate to [persons].*
- To identify a gift amount: *I give $____ to [full legal name and address of intended recipient].*
- To create a gift amount as a percentage: *I give ____ percent of my estate to [full legal name and address of intended recipient].*

In addition, your Will may designate a portion of an asset to a charity. For example: *I give 10 percent of the sale proceeds from the property located at [full address] to [full legal name and address of intended recipient].* These designations may direct funds to a charitable endowment, to a mission project, or simply to the charity. Important information, including the full name of the charity, mission project, fund, or endowment, helps your estate executor fulfill your wishes. If a similar type of mission would be an acceptable alternative should your first choice no longer be in existence, suggestions you offer provide important guidance if needed. With more than 60 percent of the United States population still reported as dying intestate,[7] building your estate plan through your Will is strongly encouraged. This stewardship discipline extends your mission work beyond your lifetime.

A Steward's Declaration

As we transition from theological grounding, financial vocabulary, and personal stewardship to congregational financial management, we reaffirm our role as stewards and the call God places on our lives using this Steward's Declaration:

> As a Christian steward, I recognize that God entrusts to us the Earth, and the fullness thereof is entrusted to us by God and that

7 http://www.aarp.org/money/investing/info-2017/half-of-adults-do-not-have-wills.html; https://news.gallup.com/poll/191651/majority-not.aspx.

we are called to be its stewards. Further I understand that our very lives come from God. Therefore, I agree to adopt these commitments and invite others to join me.

1. I commit myself to regular and responsible participation in a community of faith by attending worship and participating in study and mission activities.
2. I commit myself to personal growth and renewal through prayer, Bible study, meditation, and participation in small-group experiences.
3. I accept accountability to God, the Creator and Owner, for my treatment of the world and will strive to reduce my impact on the environment.
4. I commit myself to lead a life of creative simplicity and to share what God has entrusted to me with the world's poor.
5. I will join with others to create a more just society in which each person has access to needed resources for physical, emotional, intellectual, and spiritual growth.
6. I will be accountable to God in my occupation, and in so doing, I will seek to avoid participation in products or services that harm others.
7. I affirm God's gift of my body and commit myself to seeking physical well-being.
8. I will commit myself to examine my relations with others and act toward others with love and concern.[8]

"God Multiplies Your Gifts"

Finally, for those inspired by music and song, these lyrics from "God Multiplies Your Gifts" from *Sardines and Biscuits* sum up the personal challenges and God's promise for all stewards.

---

8 Adapted from Thomas G. Petterpiece, *Visions of a World Hungry*, quoted by Rueben P. Job and Norman Shawchuck in *A Guide to Prayer for Ministers and Other Servants* (Nashville, TN: Upper Room Books, 1983), 116–17.

God called Moses, Isaiah, and Mary to share Gifts that had
come from above.
God called Moses to lead, Isaiah to preach, and Mary to bear
goodness and love.
To bring a small piece of heaven to Earth—was the charge
gracious God gave to each–
And all said, "Thanks for asking, there are others more suited to
fulfill such a noble request.
I'm really no good." "Wait!" God spoke once again,
"You're not only good; you're the best."
There's no need to bore you with the ends of their tales.
They did as God beckoned and more:
Moses freed the oppressed, Isaiah turned loose the captives,
Mary brought good news to the poor.

REFRAIN

God multiplies your gifts. You get a liberating, elevating,
duplicating, formulated lift!
Miracles do happen all the time—and everywhere.
I gave back what I got from God. Now there's a lot to spare.

Look at the seed, it is sown to bear fruit. Yet, it doesn't know
what it will bring.
If it refuses planting it stays by itself, and from it, no new life
will spring.
God calls me to sow seeds of pardon and hope, in a world filled
with guilt and despair.
Seeds of love, faith, joy, and light, dispel hatred and doubt,
eliminate sadness and darkness.
God, I'm only one person. "Wait!" God speaks once again,
"You're not only one, you're the best!"
The story's not finished, we've a long way to go, with Yahweh
standing within us.
When we share all our gifts in praise and thanksgiving, God's
SHALOM will be the harvest.

REFRAIN

God multiplies your gifts. You get a liberating, elevating,
duplicating, formulated lift!
Miracles do happen all the time—and everywhere
I gave back what I got from God. Now there's a lot to spare!

— Words and Music by Mitchell Clyde Thomas © 1992[9]

Reflection Questions

1. Describe the largest or the greatest gift you have ever received.
2. If Jesus asked you for an accounting of your personal stewardship and generosity, how would you respond?
3. Do you turn off all the lights and electronic items when you leave a room? Why?
4. What have you learned about your personal relationship with money and how it affects our relationships with people and with God?
5. What role does generosity and responsibility to care for those in need have on your daily life? Are there examples of times when you have felt that call?
6. If God calls you today, what have you left as clues and guidance for those you leave behind? Share what you have done or need to do and when you will take your next steps. Find a family member or buddy to hold you accountable.
7. What steps would you like to take to strengthen your personal stewardship or to create a legacy that honors your life's work?
8. What are the next steps you or your church needs to take in order to be more Christ-centered stewards?

9 Used with permission. Music available for $20. To order, email Mitch.Thomas@LACLT.com.

CHAPTER FOUR

MANAGING GOD'S MONEY

Congregational Financial Stewardship

Church finances are like surgeon's tools:
they work better when they're not messed up.

—Steve Garnaas-Holmes

Accountable leadership occurs when stewards understand the financial tools for management of God's money for mission and ministry. But how can we fulfill our role as faithful stewards when we don't know exactly what we are stewarding? Balance sheets and budgets have important roles in financial stewardship, faithful accountability, and assessing financial well-being. An *assets inventory* or *balance sheet* can help us understand what we are stewards of, and a *budget* helps us determine how we are doing financially at a specific time. Looking first at how accounting systems and bank accounts support financial stewardship, this chapter defines assets and the purpose of an assets inventory or balance sheet. The second half of this chapter explores how budgets are built and managed and the role of financial reports. Leaders' use of these tools and clarity about what each one reports will strengthen everyone's understanding about financial realities.

Accounts and Accounting

Financial gifts are deposited in a bank, credit union, or other financial institution. Funds may be in one bank account or divided into multiple accounts. In most cases, missions stewarding less than $500,000 a year find one bank account meets their financial management needs. In a *unified budget* model, the operating budget and short-term designated resources are in one bank account. The treasurer tracks categories of money using an accounting system or software. In The United Methodist Church, the *Book of Discipline* allows only United Methodist Women's funds to be held separately.[1] All other funds, including trustee's funds, which are amenable to the Church Council or governing body, are stewarded by the financial leadership.

Some churches create separate bank accounts for different activities; multiple bank accounts will increase the complexity of account information to be managed. Careful assessment of bank fees and options available for nonprofit organizations—never use personal accounts—should be conducted. Multiple accounts can be avoided when precise fund descriptions within the accounting system ensure clarity and accurate bookkeeping. Consider the following financial vocabulary for clarity:

- When financial resources are held in multiple bank accounts, identify those as *accounts*.
- To identify separate activities within one bank account, use the term *fund*.
- When groups conduct specific activities or events, identify those as *projects*.
- Funds held for specific purposes are short-term *designated* or *pass-through* items. Held for a specific purpose, these funds are used before other funds and monitored to prevent an accumulation of small designated funds.

Vocabulary and definitions are important considerations when creating

1 "United Methodist Women," in *The Book of Discipline of The United Methodist Church: 2016* (Nashville, TN: Abingdon Press, 2016), ¶256.5 *Article 6. Funds—a).*

your accounting system and reports. For example, differences between Endowment Funds, which may be an account, or Memorial Funds, which may be short-term designated funds, impact how they are managed. Multiple funds and accounts increases confusion and may decrease donor confidence. Use **Worksheet 7. Financial Accounts Inventory** to assess your current accounts and future needs.

Reconciliation

The purpose of reconciling is to locate and address any errors or omissions in the internal financial management system in a timely manner. Using bank statements, each transaction, whether income and expenses, is verified. For example, does the deposit information on the first Sunday of last month match the deposit amount in the bank statement? Reconciling compares organizational financial records to bank statements, including identifying income or expense items not yet *cleared* at the financial institution. For example, a bank statement ending June 30 may not include a deposit made that day or a payment to a vendor paid on June 16 but not cashed until July 2. Simple math errors or entering a decimal point in the wrong place creates challenging puzzles when reconciling reveals differences between bank account balances and organizational financial records. Monthly reconciliation confirms accuracy regularly. This level of financial accountability inspires trust and generosity, which strengthens resources for missions.

Responsible Party/Signers

Opening a financial account requires naming at last two designated signers or contacts. *Never* open a bank account in the pastor's name or with only one member. Most banks require official documentation from the Trustees and/or the governing body, such as a Charge Conference or Church Council, to identify persons elected as signers or contact persons—including their personal contact information—to open an account.

Store the designated contact persons' information in a secure location to avoid losing track of account signers. Financial institution's legal requirements for protecting account security means they cannot disclose signers' identity. When signers' information is not available, financial institutions may give pastors access to account information, or they will provide instructions about how to provide the required verification to obtain access. The annual audit and financial review process includes verifying account signers' contact information, which should be confirmed or updated annually and recorded in a permanent file as described in chapter 9. Be aware that some missions find lost accounts in state listings of unclaimed funds.

Assets

Understanding the definition and role of assets impacts a leader's ability to assess the resilience and sustainability of your ministry. Technically, the resources stewarded for God's mission are all *assets*, including financial gifts, investments, property, and tangible goods that contribute to the organization's net worth. Assets do not include consumable items, such as paper, worship resources, educational supplies, decorations, and event or marketing resources. Some items of extraordinary worth, such as an historical silver tea service, are tangible goods, described below.

When managing financial assets, whether cash, endowments, or other investments, stewards face special responsibilities and occasional challenges. Some large assets create complexity and conflict, especially when different expectations exist. Some gifts have clear instructions from donors, such as gifts for an elevator project or parking improvements. Some have less clarity, such as the gift of a family grand piano, understood by some relatives to be on loan rather than a gift. Clear documentation ensures assets are used as intended and provides stewards with important information over the years. Accurate communication, education, and information help people understand, for example, that endowment funds supplement specific missions and don't replace regular giving. In some cases, documentation clarifying a gift's purpose and use is set by the donor through gift documentation in a will. If you are named in a will, the executor or attorney will contact you. One donor stipulated that her gift could not be accessed by her church until the next generation reached maturity. The bank stewarding her gift determined the age of maturity as twenty years and distributed the $1,000,000 asset, which had grown to over $2,300,000 on the twentieth anniversary of this gift.[2]

---

2 Shared by Rev. Althea Jackson, East Providence United Methodist Church, East Providence, RI. Used with permission.

Acceptance of Gifts and Documentation

Assets are often larger gifts that have an important review and acceptance process. When a donor's wishes align with your mission, gifts are accepted. If the donor's wishes do not align with your mission or violate your polity, the gift should be renegotiated or refused. The trustees, endowment committees, and pastors are responsible for assessing and evaluating gifts and reporting their recommendations for action by the governing body: Charge Conference. Action by the Charge Conference is one accountability step ensuring major gifts are recorded in official records of your mission.

Gifts received without guidance from the donor are considered *undesignated* or *unrestricted. Unrestricted* gifts' use is determined by the recipient, making this a popular type of gift for your mission. Unrestricted gifts also trigger differing hopes and visions by leaders, sometimes causing conflicts regarding priorities and preferences. Destructive conflict may erupt when, for example, some leaders value the steeple repairs over expanding mission work and vice versa. Because both needs are valid, these types of conflict are painful and unhealthy. I visited a highly conflicted congregation and asked each of the approximately twenty-five persons present to explain the situation using a covenant circle process. Perspectives shared included both protecting the endowed funding of a full-time pastoral salary and concerns about critical damage to the building's foundation. Emotions and opinions flowed freely. Before the last person shared her perspective, one person asked if the endowment was large enough to cover the building repair work and still generate enough revenue to fund the pastor's salary. After quickly running some numbers, they discovered the answer was yes! The intervention of a mediator helped them discover they really didn't have a problem, unfortunately after weeks of conflict and hurt. Is your mission experiencing enough transparency about its assets to prevent a situation like this from occurring?

Establishing a gift-acceptance policy and endowment policy describing plans and priorities regarding assets reduces conflicts. An endowment policy that sets missional priorities before the endowment receives any gifts provides clarity and reduces conflict, which others' generosity inadvertently triggers. If your answer to any of the following questions is no, consider creating or reviewing these documents as soon as possible.

- Do you have a gift-acceptance policy?
- Do you have an endowment policy that sets priorities for planned or significant gifts?
- If one or both policies exist, are they useful and are leaders familiar with their content?

See chapter 9 and appendices for additional information on these policies.

Remember, all assets are reported in the annual audit and balance sheet. Nonprofit organizations report all funds, bank accounts, stocks, bonds, or any investment accounts annually, including those designated as endowments or trustee's funds. No funds by any subgroup are exempt from this requirement. United Methodist churches and missions are currently exempt from the federal IRS filing requirements (Form 990) due to a group exemption verified by private letter ruling. The private letter ruling document verifies nonprofit status for some grant applications and local sales or property tax status. However, this filing exemption does not waive accountability to donors, other governmental agencies, or one another, including the expectation of an annual audit balance sheet reporting all financial resources.

Cash

Many gifts to missions are made by cash, check, or another form of funds transfer from one financial institution to another. While we often think of assets only as invested funds or accumulated savings, cash gifts also are assets. Special savings accounts or certificates of deposit purchased for greater interest earnings or set-aside resources for a rainy day are all assets for your mission. The funds in bank accounts may be designated for the current budget; however, they are also counted as assets in both the audit and the balance sheet described in more detail below.

Investments

Investments are a form of assets managed by another financial institution on your behalf. Because over time investments—which typically include bonds and equities, or stocks—offer a greater return through interest or dividend payments, investment can have a positive impact on your income, again, over time. Because these financial options are not as protected as many bank accounts, investment income should not be more than 30 percent of your total income and should be used to supplement your mission.

Some planned gifts benefitting your mission in the future may also be invested. Donors may or may not disclose a planned gift, so the potential value, or even existence, of some assets may not be fully known. Careful documentation of assets and any disclosed planned gifts provides future generations with valuable information.

Property

Property includes physical buildings—church, parsonage, mission sites—and land, such as parking lot, fields, and undeveloped space that you own, manage, or lease for missional use. Property has a tax valuation, an insurance valuation, which may represent full replacement value or a partial replacement value based on what would be rebuilt, and a real estate value representing the potential value if sold. These values may vary significantly, and obtaining all three values for comparative purposes is useful. Consider making a pictorial inventory to record important information about property descriptions and conditions, and keep in mind that insurance may provide coverage for certain losses or damages. Maintaining property for safety and funding short-term and long-term maintenance is expected.

Tangible Goods

Tangible goods are physical items such as Communion service sets or crosses; musical instruments, such as pianos or the organ; kitchen equipment, such as stoves, refrigerators, and microwave ovens; office equipment, including copiers, computers, and projection equipment; furnishings, such as tables, chairs, pews, couches, and other physical equipment. These items are not *consumable* and could potentially be liquidated or sold. Some lose value, or *depreciate*, over time, so strategic budget planning may consider the life expectancy of some of these items—copiers, computers, boilers—and could create reserve funds in anticipation of future capital replacement costs. A pictorial summary is also valuable should any of these items need to be replaced due to theft, fire, flood, or other disaster.

Some tangible goods have extraordinary value and may warrant additional insurance coverage through an insurance rider at additional cost. One church discovered the angel Gabriel statue on their steeple was gold and eventually sold it to the Smithsonian Institute; another purchased additional insurance for their exquisite sanctuary chandelier valued at $800,000. Some tangible goods will rise or fall in value, and a detailed inventory provides useful documentation. Many tangible goods will not be included in your balance sheet, but an inventory for insurance purposes could be very valuable. See **Worksheet 8** to begin creating your Assets Inventory.

Balance Sheet: Reporting Net Worth and Assets Inventory

Providing a summary of all assets, including money in all accounts and property values, a *balance sheet* is reported at least annually to finance leadership and reviewed or created during the annual financial review or audit. Leaders steward all gifts God has provided for their mission work in addition to monitoring the annual budget. Some missions steward millions of invested dollars, while others use resources that should be safeguarded for future generations. The best way to obtain a comprehensive understanding of the financial health of your mission is to create and review an assets inventory and a balance sheet.

The purpose of the balance sheet is to identify all resources and financial obligations. While a budget focuses on the financial position at a specific time, the *balance sheet* identifies all resources, including investments, property, valuable tangible goods, and funds, as well as all obligations, such as loans, tax obligations, and debts, including arrearages, such as unpaid insurance premiums or denominational connectional support commitments known in The United Methodist Church as apportionments or mission shares. The balance sheet more accurately reveals the vulnerability of your mission when, for example, a budget report may not report thousands of dollars in arrearages or loans. A balance sheet also reveals the relative health of a mission struggling to balance the budget while protecting rather than spending thousands of dollars in investments. The assets inventory or balance sheet is a vital component of the stewardship assessment of your mission work. Balance sheet reports generated using financial software packages require careful review to ensure the report contains all the information needed for complete financial clarity. The balance sheet gives leaders a holistic view of financial resources and responsibilities and improves decision making. Finance leadership needs to review a balance sheet because it provides a lot more information about the mission's financial health than a budget report.

In **Figure 1**, this mission's current balance sheet summary indicates that they have taken on some debt and used some of their designated funds. The resulting adjustments show that they have either invested in some missional expansion endeavors or that they have taken on debt to supplement their operations or to fulfill some connectional commitments (arrearages). The first option is exciting; the second suggests the possibility of unhealthy preservation attempts. While the total fund balance has shifted by only $5,000, the underlying changes may indicate very different financial positions.

	Current Budget Period	**Previous Budget Period**
Assets		
Operations Fund	$23,000	$18,000
Designated Funds	$14,000	$25,000
Property	$175,000	$175,000
Endowment/Investments	$7,500	$5,500
Equipment	$6,000	$7,000
Assets Total	$225,500	$230,500
Liabilities		
Accounts Payable	$16,000	$17,500
Loan	$65,000	0
Arrearages	$10,000	$40,000
Net Assets		
Unrestricted	$129,000	$167,500
Restricted	$5,500	$5,500
Total Net Assets	$134,500	$173,000
Total Net Assets and Liabilities	$225,500	$230,500

Figure 1: Sample Balance Sheet

Worksheet 9 offers an assets inventory format to document the assets stewarded by your mission and a modified balance sheet exercise. Supplement a balance sheet's accounting information with additional background on your assets using this inventory format for more detailed recordkeeping and clarity about the financial health of your mission.

Budget

A budget is the internal recordkeeping system for tracking current financial activity. Simple ledgers, accounting software, or sophisticated databases track this financial information. Some software programs also track attendance, program registrations, or other demographic or statistical information. Computer literacy as well as financial complexity and budget size will affect your choice in selecting an accounting system, which will be customized by each user. Many missions have computerized their financial work, and even small-membership churches are encouraged to use software to simplify math and data management. This financial accounting system creates a supplement to the financial information provided by banks, credit unions, or other financial institutions that manage your funds. Accounting systems typically include an *operating fund* for current expenses, sometime broken into committees or ministry area budgets, and *designated funds* for specific programs, activities, or missions. Some missions create additional funds, but the funds tracking capabilities built into software programs may be sufficient.

A budget is more than a list of numbers. This tool for tracking financial activity is a faith statement describing your mission and priorities. Budgets provide information about ministry, mission activities, and accompanying financial obligations. The primary purpose, however, is factual documentation of financial goals and transactions. We adopt a budget, typically annually, to establish our financial goals and commitments. A budget is also time-limited, documenting the financial transactions during the designated time. In addition, official adoption of the budget establishes amounts the treasurer is authorized to pay toward expenses and financial commitments during the budget time period.

Leader comfort and competence with budgets and what a budget communicates, or hides, affects our mission efforts. The numbers create a ministry plan for tracking income and expenditures during the budget time period. Financial reports show progress on income and expenses and whether the budget runs from January to December or July to June; complete reports show leaders whether the income is greater than, less than, or equal to the expenditures. The *bottom line* is the result of subtracting expenditures from the income. Using *line items* to describe types of income and expenses, leaders see progress and changes over time. Line items describe types of income, such as pledges, special offerings, or distributions from invested funds and expenses, such as salaries, utilities, or programs. **Figure 2** offers a simple budget example.

Faithful Followers Mission	**Budget 12 Months**
Income	
Pledges and Regular Giving	$95,000
Building Shared Users	$12,000
Other Income/Investments	$1,000
Income Total	$108,000
Expenses	
Personnel	$65,000
Property	$8,000
Program	$6,000
Administration/Communication	$5,000
Connectional Commitment	$24,000
Expense Total	$108,000
Bank Balance January 1	$15,000

Figure 2. Simple Budget Example

An accurate, detailed, and understandable budget summarizes what your mission is doing and its current priorities. While budgets support financial management and accountability, they may also limit mission. In some cases, upon adoption, leaders forget the importance of regularly monitoring and evaluating the budget. New mission opportunities can be delayed until the next budget cycle, and unexpected expenses may lead to anxiety and internal conflict. Budget adjustments may seem complicated, but in some cases, adjustments serve the mission well. When the top priority becomes preserving the budget as adopted at all costs, the focus shifts from mission to preservation, reducing the budget's usefulness. Primarily designed for accountability, a budget should inform decision making, not mandate the future. Growing organizations realize budgets are thermometers, most useful if they are shaken down occasionally, as they may need to be recalibrated! At the same time, budgets prevent financial chaos by setting goals, revealing changing needs, and monitoring financial positions.

Designated or Pass-Through Funds

Designated funds created by an organization range from coffee funds to camp scholarships to invested endowments. Short-term designated funds are tracked to ensure their use aligns with their original purpose. Short-term designated funds hold money to be distributed promptly (for example, retreat registrations, a special offering for a natural disaster, or a youth-led community service project). Their purpose is *designated* to honor the giver's intent and ensure funds are not used for general expenses. Because these funds *pass through* the financial system, they are tracked by the treasurer and distributed according to instructions. Resisting the temptation to temporarily borrow against these funds for immediate cash-flow needs is strongly encouraged. Treasurers facing financial shortfalls should report the situation to the finance leadership for collaborative efforts to address the needs. For more information on cash flow, see chapter 6.

Building a Budget

A budget presentation to the governing body for their consideration and adoption includes:

- a summary of actual expenditures for the previous period (year-to-date or year-end estimate);
- an estimate of projected income for the next budget period; and
- the proposed expenditures for the next budget period. This is the portion of the budget presentation adopted.

Clues about current health and financial resilience exist in the previous year's actual income and expenses information. The goal of the budget-building process is a budget proposal where income plus carryover funds available from the previous budget equals the proposed expenses: a *balanced* budget.

Prior to disclosing the proposed budget or presenting it for adoption, finance leaders are strongly urged to complete a generosity-based commitment process described more fully in the next chapter. Completing this stewardship discipline before adopting the budget focuses giving commitments on gratitude to God and appreciation for the mission, preventing an unhealthy calculation of a per-member share of the proposed budget. When held before the budget is presented, a second round of commitment invitations could improve the financial situation. Sometimes a new ministry is possible based on commitment responses. Options increase for finance leadership to align anticipated income with desired expenditures when the proposed budget is presented *after* a commitment process.

Creating a budget with broad categories summarizing groups of more detailed line items allows increased flexibility for budget management. If budget categories are adopted, funds may move between the category's line items when needed. Broad categories, such as utilities (electric, gas, water, phone, and Internet costs), gives budgetary flexibility for these line items. Or a $2,000 Christian Education budget might include multiple line items, such as supplies, events, and training. Approval from the governing body is not needed for internal category adjustments. Following the example of **Figure 3**, a Property budget category could include utilities, heating/cooling, maintenance, and water. In many settings, these broad categories are sufficient for the governing body, and the more detailed line items support the finance leadership's budget monitoring work.

Categories	Line Items	Budget Adopted	Budget Line Items
Education			$4,000
	Curriculum Supplies Promotional Materials Vacation Bible School		$1,500 $1,000 $500 $1,000
Property			$25,000
	Electric Gas Water Phone Internet/Webpage		$10,000 $8,000 $4,000 $1,800 $1,200
Worship			$7,000
	Guest Preachers Guest Musicians Supplies Bibles		$1,500 $1,000 $3,000 $1,500

Figure 3: Sample Budget Categories

Remember to include all financial commitments and obligations in the proposed budget. Budgeting only a portion of connectional commitments to balance the budget breaks our covenantal and connectional commitments, surely not compatible with our generosity and accountability goals. Build a complete budget, even if funding it is going to be a challenge. See chapter 5 for more resources on funding your missions. Your budget plan should include the following financial categories and items.

- *Personnel/Staff* includes compensation, insurances, benefits, reimbursed expenses, retirement, and taxes, plus moving expenses and sabbatical funds.
- *Property* includes mortgage or loan payments, maintenance—long-term and short-term—and improvements, utilities, insurance, and applicable taxes.
- *Program* includes worship, education, mission, outreach, music, events, trips, scholarships, and other nurture-outreach-witness activities. Rather

than creating a separate mission category, identify all budget categories as missional.

- *Infrastructure* includes communications and technology, marketing, online giving services, computers and software, resources.
- *Connectional Commitments*, also known as apportionments, missional giving, or mission shares, are funds submitted for denominational or conference ministries typically beyond your local setting. Direct billing of pension, health insurance, or other costs may be included here or in Personnel/Staff.
- Finally, include end-of-year *carryover*, either positive or negative. This adds additional clarity to the financial situation.

Congregations have a responsibility to budget faithfully. The *budget-building process* outlined here, and in more detail in **Worksheet 10**, helps finance leaders and Church Council/Administrative Boards "ensure adequate provision for the financial needs of the church."[3]

The financial secretary provides an income projection, taking into consideration the previous year's actual income records and any anticipated changes. The financial secretary incorporates any other factors that cause confidence or caution about giving capacity into the income projection.

INCOME PROJECTION ASSESSMENT

Using the financial secretary's statistics, consider the following characteristics of your donor base and how they impact your financial resilience or vulnerability.

1. Consider the number of giving units as a percentage of your total participants or supporters.
2. Consider the number of contributors who are funding 80 percent of the budget.
3. Consider the number of contributors who are funding 50 percent of the budget.

3 "Church Council," in *The Discipline*, ¶252.4c.

4. Consider the average age or life stage of those who give regularly.
5. Evaluate whether your income is dependent on a small number of giving units or spread out over a broad group of supporters from different age groups.

Expense requests for the next budget are then collected in consultation with appropriate bodies. In The United Methodist Church, all budget requests are subject to review by the finance leadership, except for the pastoral compensation agreement, which is negotiated by the Pastor/Staff Relations Committee and the pastor for submission to the budget-building process. After receiving requests from ministry areas, build the expense budget projection using any of the following techniques:

- *Bottom-up* budget building is based on the previous year's allocations and actual expenses, thereby holding groups accountable for their activities. This model is also described as "Use It or Lose It!"
- *Top-down* budgeting assesses income and distributes it over funding areas. This model causes everyone to feel their work is underfunded or compromised but creates a budget that is considered safe or reasonable.
- *Zero-based* budgeting offers no guarantees based on previous year's funding, and each area sets goals and advocates for financial support, creating accountability and sometimes unhealthy competition.
- *A combination* of all or some of these methods designed to suit your needs.

Expense projections include the full amount of connectional commitments or apportionments due or in arrears to keep track of these liabilities. Include the value of donations from professionals who donate their services (for example, a volunteer organist). This provides clarity about total expenses and needs when that donation ends.

Once the income and expense projections are completed, compare the two to determine if the proposed expense budget is equal to, greater than, or less than the projected income. If there is a gap between requested expenses and projected income, take some time to reflect on all the numbers collected and the mission priorities as well as your stewardship culture. The process of transforming funding requests into a budget proposal can challenge our faith and requires clarifying conversations and accountability. Budget balancing conversations and negotiations generate anxiety, so they should be held in a setting appropriate for sacred deliberations. Discernment with trust in God's provision helps stewards honor God's will. Finance leaders may prefer conservative income projections and generous expense projections, while the stewardship mind-set requires occasional leaps of faith. Balancing reality with possibility and the differences between a financial mind-set and stewardship visions influences the budget-building process. Serving as stewards of God's mission, rather than as gatekeepers or naysayers, is a healthier role for finance leaders.

The finance leadership and Church Council are responsible for ensuring adequate funding for the mission and obligated to create a funding plan for the proposed expenditures, if needed. This plan should be created, presented, and adopted before the budget is approved when a plan to build revenue is needed. Budget approval authority belongs to the governing body, meeting as a Charge Conference; this ensures broad input and ownership for the budget plans. Once a budget is adopted, the real stewardship work begins. The line item budget used by the finance leadership should be available upon request, but it doesn't need to be shared with everyone. Chapter 8 describes some positive options for communication, affirmation, and encouragement. Finally, remember that a budget is a tool for your missions, but it is only one of your stewardship tools.

Deficit Budget

Some congregations adopt a budget with expenditures greater than anticipated income. Sometimes considering a *deficit budget* challenges people to try new stewardship activities to grow giving generosity. At other times, it is an avoidance strategy or causes austerity practices that can negatively impact mission. Larger organizations may adopt a budget with a small variance 3 to 5 percent, representing possible fluctuations in revenue and expenditures during the year without using the deficit budget terminology. In other situations, the deficit budget practice has unintended costs, including creating a negative self-image. The budget gap will be filled either by dipping into savings or assets, by reducing expenditures, or by last-minute, end-of-year gifts. In some cases, albeit not a best practice, a donor asks what is needed and funds the difference.

All these scenarios have one thing in common: they create a culture of failure for the members and community. Avoid this ineffective messaging by resisting the temptation to adopt a deficit budget. Honestly sharing how missions will be funded during the budget period, even if that requires liquidating assets, will motivate more generosity than adopting a budget with failure built in.

Speaking the truth in love is challenging, but it is healthier to share that the current income projection is going to require added assets than to keep that information secret in order to avoid anxiety. Is it better to reduce staff to balance the budget or to institute a second commitment process? Is telling people the budget is fully funded going to inspire or reduce generosity? The answer lies in how information is shared. Guilt and complaining are counterproductive and discourage giving. Confident and inspiring communication is often the ingredient for stewardship miracles.

"I ASKED!"

Pastor Rosanne communicated confidently to her congregation that meeting all their financial obligations would be possible if they could increase their revenue by 10 percent.

The congregation responded to this positive and challenging invitation. In addition, a donor presented a gift of $20,000 as an expression of gratitude for the church and its commitment to be a spiritual presence in the community.[4]

Donors respect honesty and are waiting to hear they are needed. Are you telling your donors how important they are and the difference they make?

4 As told by Rev. Rosanne Roberts, First United Methodist Church of Hudson, MA. Used with permission.

Many donors are waiting to be asked. Build your budget with the knowledge that anything is possible with God, acknowledging that we often don't ask clearly. Even worse, when donors experience an incomplete or misleading report about finances, trust and generosity diminish.

Prefunded Budget Model

When revenue for the current budget's expenditures are raised the previous year, the current budget's income is available in advance. In a prefunded budget model, income generated in the current budget period funds the next year's mission work. Several decades ago, the North Carolina Annual Conference of The United Methodist Church strategically generated additional resources over several years to build up enough reserves to create a prefunded budget. The financial resources for the current year were already secured.[5] Because current expenditures are paid with income received in the previous year, fundraising energy and stewardship shifts to the next year's visions. As funds for the next year's mission are received, they may generate additional revenue through interest and investment returns. What would need to occur for your ministry to make this strategic shift?

Financial Reports

Periodic financial reports communicate financial status and progress toward budgetary goals. The budget report reveals over and under expenditures and when unexpected costs arise; a budget review explores options for adjusting resources to meet emerging needs. Because some people are uncomfortable with numbers or with financial accountability, budget reports with huge amounts of data or partial reporting reduce generosity and cause confusion. Financial reports may also mislead leaders when unpaid bills aren't reported. Ensuring your financial reports communicate fully and clearly impacts your financial stewardship and culture of generosity. Financial reports are for communication, so make sure they communicate well.

Financial reports provide data for budget evaluations. Periodic financial

---

5 See budget report in *North Carolina Annual Conference 2017 Journal*, including previous year actual expenditures, current year funded budget, and funds to be raised in current year for the next year, https://nccumc.org/secretary/files/Journal-2017-1.pdf, 197–202.

reports contribute to mission assessment and wise decision making by providing updates on assumptions and information, aligning plans with reality. Also known as *profit and loss statements*, the periodic budget reports show income and expenses during a period of time within the budget cycle, typically monthly or quarterly. During a financial shortfall, more frequent financial reports may become necessary.

Complete and comprehensive budget reports summarize the actual financial activity, the adopted budget, and current bank account balances. Progress toward the adopted budget in actual amounts or percentages is also often included. The sample in **Figure 4** uses broad categories to simplify reporting and includes bank account information to summarize financial activity year to date. Note that the change in the bank balance matches the financial report's balance amount. Also note that this sample report could be healthy in April but raises some serious questions if it is for September. The Budget Year-to-Date amount suggests that this report may be for June. Do you see why? See **Worksheet 11. Financial Report Review** to explore some other clues.

	Actual Year-to-Date	Budget Total	Budget Year-to-Date (50%)	YTD % Actual
Income				
Offerings	$60,500	$120,000	$60,000	50%
Monthly Dinners	$3,100	$10,000	$5,000	31%
Investments	$1,200	$4,000	$2,000	30%
Weddings	$1,000	$1,000	$500	100%
Building Users		$20,000	$10,000	0%
Carryover	$1,000	$ 1,000	$500	100%
Income Total	$66,800	$156,000	$78,000	43%
Expenses				
Worship	$180	$200	$100	90%
Programs	$900	$700	$350	129%
Property	$6,400	$12,400	$6,200	52%

	Actual Year-to-Date	Budget Total	Budget Year-to-Date (50%)	YTD % Actual
Missions	$1,000	$2,000	$1,000	50%
Personnel	$37,400	$75,000	$37,500	50%
Insurance & Benefits	$12,000	$25,000	$12,500	48%
Maintenance	$8,000	$11,000	$5,500	73%
Apportionments	$11,000	$23,000	$11,500	48%
Expenses Total	$78,880	$149,300	$74,650	53%
Balance (deficit)	($10,080)	$6,700	$3,350	–150%
Faithful Funds Bank (Operations)				
Beginning Balance	$18,870			
Ending Balance	$8,700			
Designated Funds	$4,800			

Figure 4: Financial Report Sample

Projection Adjustments

Adjustments to budget projections, acknowledging repeating financial fluctuations in giving or expense patterns, can be integrated into financial reports. For example, consider the monthly income projection, which is typically broken into twelve equal amounts for the budget year. Yet we know that income fluctuates greatly from month to month due to seasonal changes and population movement north or south (the snowbird effect). A straight-line projection often causes monthly income reports to fall behind expenses most of the year, creating reports that will depress generosity.

Adjusting monthly projections to reflect long-standing income patterns improves monthly financial reports. For example, an Adjusted Monthly Income Projection could assign 8 percent of the expected income each month from January to June and September through November; 4 percent to July and August; and the remaining 20 percent to the month of December (see **Figure 5**). An adjusted income projection acknowledges the flow of income during the year and sets experience-based goals by reviewing income patterns during previous years. An adjusted monthly projection also promotes generosity by creating a more positive financial report. Review financial patterns from the last three to five years to identify reasonable giving patterns for adjusting projections. Any adjustments implemented should be explained clearly. Adjustments that reduce negative reporting will motivate generosity.

January	8%	$8,000
February	8%	$8,000
March	8%	$8,000
April	8%	$8,000
May	8%	$8,000
June	8%	$8,000
July	4%	$4,000
August	4%	$4,000
September	8%	$8,000
October	8%	$8,000
November	8%	$8,000
December	20%	$20,000

Figure 5: Adjusted Monthly Projections,
$100,000 Income Budget Example

In summary, remember that budget building and management work is sacred and will directly impact the morale and confidence of the whole community. Healthy missions cultivate generosity, communicate honestly and positively about finances, and honor our commitment to serve all through our discipleship, sharing the love of God with all persons in all places at all times.[6]

Reflection Questions

1. How can you more fully communicate church finances? How might that inspire generosity?

6 For a more comprehensive exploration of church finances and additional aspects of accounting principles, see Janet and Phil Jamieson, *Ministry and Money: A Practical Guide for Pastors* (Louisville: Westminster John Knox, 2009), which expands this topic especially for larger missions.

2. Describe the most interesting thing you have learned about financial reports and budgets.
3. If Jesus asked what you are doing with God's blessings, what would your financial reports tell him?
4. In your experience, what are the connections between budgets, financial management, and generosity?
5. What additional training might your financial team need?
6. Explore ways your finances, budget, and reports strengthen or weaken generosity. Identify ways you might improve.

CHAPTER FIVE

INCOME AND MOTIVATING GENEROSITY

A painter understands oils
not for the paint, but for the art.
A good steward understands money,
not for the money, but for the possibilities.

—Steve Garnaas-Holmes

Then Moses gave an order and they sent this word throughout the camp: "No man or woman is to make anything else as an offering for the sanctuary." And so the people were restrained from bringing more, because what they already had was more than enough to do all the work.

—Exodus 36:6-7

Success stories have one common element: someone asked and people responded. Money for mission multiplies when people joyfully share their gifts. We praise Jesus for the miraculous feeding of five thousand on the Bethsaida hillside (Matthew 14:13-21), but what if the real miracle was enlisting the crowd to share their gifts with one another? What if our responsibility to accurately count and account for income could also inspire and motivate generosity? Our motivations to give include gratitude to God, the joy of giving, awareness of a need, passions and interests, life-long commitments, desire to positively impact the lives of others, and the satisfaction of being acknowledged and known as a generous, helpful person or church.

Research on philanthropy cites eight charitable giving motivations: (a) awareness of need, (b) solicitation, (c) costs and benefits, (d) altruism, (e) reputation, (f) psychological benefits, (g) values, and (h) efficacy.[1] Expectations about reporting the impact of gifts and the mission they support are increasing. And leadership that focuses on generosity can positively affect our mission capacity. When we don't invite others, we miss opportunities and deprive others of being part of God's vision. Leaders with a vision invite others to join them. That invitation is known as an *ask*. The purpose of an *ask* is to enlist people in the mission. Discovering others' visions by exploring mission alignment, shared interests, capacity, and readiness to support your mission precedes an ask. Like any pastoral care, this listening takes time and observation skills. Whether simply inviting a person or group to join you in supporting a mission effort or a more strategic relationship cultivation process, the goal of creating a new partnership or empowering others to create their legacy or support a vision must be your motivation. Tips and coaching on asking are also valuable, or you might find inspiration in the Nike slogan, *Just do it*. On the one hand, good observation skills about lifestyle, jobs, and hobbies offer clues for leaders seeking to cultivate resources for mission. On the other hand, significant capacity is often hidden or lost when, for example, elderly members fall off visitation lists and leaders forget to introduce new pastors to all members. The fact that most large bequests are a total surprise suggests how unobservant we actually are and how little we know each other.

One of my ask-coaching mantras is, "You know more than you think you know." We often assume we know nothing about another's capacity to be generous. At one extreme, exceedingly frugal individuals are often good savers, whose disciplines enable them to accomplish their goals to bless others

---

1 René Bekkers and Pamala Wiepking, "A Literature Review of Empirical Studies of Philanthropy: Eight Mechanisms That Drive Charitable Giving," *Nonprofit and Voluntary Sector Quarterly* 40, no. 5 (2011): 924–73; http://www.wiepking.com/papers/BekkersWiepking_2011_NVSQ.pdf.

at some point in time. At the other extreme, persons who travel frequently, have new cars every few years, or trade up for the latest phone or new technologies are offering clues about their potential capacity to be leaders in your mission. Retirees on a fixed income may have greater financial flexibility than parents of college students. The most common mistake leaders repeatedly make—that is guaranteed to limit your mission—is the assumption that others don't want to be asked. Any mission worth doing is worth supporting, and we diminish the leadership capacity of others when we assume they won't be interested.

Our personal attitudes and the culture of communication and generosity we create may be the first step toward increasing missional stewardship. Bearing in mind that many factors, including our mind-set, will influence giving, we turn now to more technical skills for generating and maximizing income, money for mission.

Gift Acceptance

The gift acceptance process protects both givers and receivers. A gift is freely given, which means that the donor relinquishes all control over the gift upon completion. Clarifying conversation prior to completion of the gift helps set boundaries, especially with more significant gifts. The purpose of these boundaries is to protect donors from potential tax implications and conflict of interest issues, both of which reduce generosity when things go wrong. All donors deserve clarity about their rights and privileges as well as protection from accusations or perceptions of using their gifts to influence decisions and missional governance.

Trustee responsibilities include reviewing larger gifts and bequests to determine their acceptance or rejection. Gifts made through bequests and planned gift instruments, such as gift annuities or trusts, should be reviewed by the Trustees or Endowment leadership before their acceptance, which is then recorded in the official minutes of the Charge Conference. This review ensures that gifts align with the values and principles of your mission. Gifts that are inappropriate or that have potential hidden costs are not accepted. For example, the gift of a home that needs extensive repair, or property with prior use as a laundromat or gas station, may lead to mission-threatening costs and heartache. Some people creatively debate the pros and cons of gifts resulting from raffles, even though they are excluded by our United Methodist social principles. Adopting policies for gift acceptance is the clearest way to establish expectations and boundaries, while at the same time giving donors helpful information and encouraging their generosity.

Acknowledgment and Substantiation

Stewarding others' generosity places certain responsibilities on those receiving financial or tangible gifts. Missions need leaders aware of the responsibilities of receiving donated funds, especially as laws affecting nonprofit status and donations vary. Your mission has complete control over gifts received and must manage gift acceptance documentation carefully. All gifts deserve confirmation and gratitude; some gifts need specific types of acknowledgment, also known as substantiation. Gifts that impact personal income taxes require substantiation, a written statement from the recipient for the donor's financial records. To provide this, use letterhead stationary and state the amount of a monetary gift or provide a description of donated items without stating a monetary value. Donors are responsible for determining the eligibility and monetary value of donated items. Online donation-valuation guides help donors to price nonmonetary gifts. In addition, gift acknowledgment letters must include the phrase "no goods or services were received" by the donor. Sample substantiation letters are available online. Review tax guidance or seek legal counsel for other restrictions on gifts to be aware of limitations and tax implications.

A HARD LESSON

A dedicated leader who knew the financial challenges of the church decided to help by donating paper supplies. He faithfully kept his receipts for his taxes. Unfortunately, when audited, the IRS denied $450 of those donations because he didn't have a gift acknowledgment letter from the church. How can you help your members be more aware of the risks and documentation needed for tax deduction eligibility?

Nonprofits that proactively provide gift substantiation and acknowledgment letters to donors model donor-centric stewardship. Substantiation letters document donations of food for community meals and even bake-sale fudge as qualified charitable contributions. In addition, winning bidders of auction items may itemize the portion of their winning bid that exceeds the value of the item. Being generous has multiple benefits as we bless generous people.

Undesignated or Unrestricted Gifts vs. Designated or Restricted Gifts

Gifts received without any suggestions for their use are considered *undesignated* or *unrestricted*. These gifts have the most flexibility. However, as donors become increasingly interested in knowing how their gifts are used, they may indicate a desired intent by offering restricted gifts. *Restrictions* are conditions donors put on gifts. *Designations* are purposes selected by the receiving organization. Both terms place obligations on gifts and should be carefully communicated and documented to avoid future confusion. Corporate memory is usually brief, and disagreements about the use of Sister Alice's bequest in 1920 might be very painful!

Let's consider a donor's perspective first: restricted gifts may be offered for a specific purpose (for example, for educational scholarships or capital expenses, such as a new roof). Other restriction examples include a gift from Mrs. Soprano for choir robes, funds from Mr. Toyota to repair the parking lot, or gifts from the Birch family to send six youth to summer camp. If the restriction is too limiting or unacceptable for your mission, consider conversation about broadening the restrictions. For example, a gift restricted by a donor to replace pew cushions could be expanded to other worship ministry purposes. When the donor and recipient agree to an identified restriction, the gift is made and immediately becomes a designated gift or part of a designated fund with a note about the appropriate purpose.

WARNING! Certain restrictions may limit the tax benefit for donors or be ethically questionable. For example, a gift to a scholarship fund from which the donor can authorize a scholarship to a family member creates a conflict of interest. Gifts for a project the mission cannot legally conduct have serious implications. When restrictions are not appropriate, gifts should not be accepted. The gift review and agreement process is critical because the gift will become part of your mission. Donors must work with leadership to find an acceptable agreement. Again, donor-restricted gifts require review and consultation to make sure that donor and recipient wishes and needs are considered. When a mission chooses to create a new designated fund with a gift aligned with its goals, the gift becomes a lead commitment for new ventures or ministries. Honest conversation increases communication and trust, which, in turn, encourages generosity.

> ***True Story***: For a number of years a donor made annual gifts to his favorite project, a dishwasher fund. The church didn't create a dishwasher fund, but the financial secretary didn't want to hurt the feelings of the donor.
>
> Then when the trustees inquire about installing a dishwasher, the town rules that the property is a wetlands zone, thereby preventing a dishwasher installation. The donor's restricted gifts are deemed to be unusable forever.
>
> What went wrong, and what are the church's options?

Churches need to identify specific needs or projects aligned with their goals and priorities. The governing body may create designated funds to collect gifts for a mission project, for a building project such as handicap bathroom or roof repairs, or for a scholarship fund. Some designated funds are short-term, such as a mission trip fund or mission appeal campaign, while others are longer term, such as a memorial fund or an ongoing youth group activity fund.

Designations are created by the organization, so they can also be dissolved or redistributed as long as donor-restricted funds are used for the purposes accepted. Designated funds that contain only gifts from unidentified donors can be used as the mission wishes. For example, funds designated by the Finance Committee from an undesignated offering for a mission trip may be reallocated by the Finance Committee for another purpose if the mission trip funds are not needed for that project. However, when donors to a designated fund are identified, their input or per-

mission may be needed before funds are redesignated. Donors or living family members may be consulted for written authorization to redesignate their initially restricted gift. In some cases, redirecting previously accepted restricted gifts may require requesting court review and approval. Documentation of purpose and contributions to each designated fund is thus very important.

Finally, remember that an undesignated or unrestricted gift may be used for any purpose—the most useful and flexible type of gift. Churches find undesignated gifts most appealing, while donors may prefer to offer suggestions about the use of their gifts. Managing this natural tension keeps leaders on their toes, balancing their wishes with motivating donors' generosity. Because memories are fickle and fleeting, careful documentation of the classification of a gift, including designated or undesignated and any accepted donor restrictions, is critical to building trust and integrity with donors.

Now that we have clarified the types of gifts organizations receive, let's look at the sources of income to consider when building an income projection for the budget.

Income Projection

An income projection describes the anticipated contributions or revenue from all sources expected during a period of time. This includes all anticipated sources of income or revenue for well-informed planning. Assess your income projections carefully. Pledges, a common source of mission income, may not come in at 100 percent each year. A percentage for *slippage* built into the income projection addresses this gap between pledge amounts and actual income. In addition, decisions to use reserves or invested funds, which reduce future interest income, impacts other income-generating potential.

When anticipated sources of income are clearly identified in the income projection, the financial secretary can easily identify and report income projection changes during the year. Supplemental income can be channeled into new mission work or build up emergency reserves. Monitoring income activity continues throughout the budget period because increases or decreases in contributions may lead to adjustments in previously approved expenditures. Whenever income numbers are adjusted to reflect new information or to balance the budget, explanatory notes help others understand these adjustments.

Carryover or End-of-Year Balances

Some churches focus only on the current budget period when reviewing their financial status. Each year will have an ending balance, either positive or negative, which should be included in the current period's income projection. End-of-year balances vary greatly depending on actual income and expenditures, which seldom exactly match the budget projections. If negative, either reserves or assets are often used to cover expenditures. If positive, this income is available to build reserves, for additional mission work, or to carry into the next year. The end-of-year balance or carryover should be included as a line item in the income projection, even if it is then set aside for operating reserves.

Multiple Spigots Theory

Where does your income come from? Imagine filling a tub with water using one faucet. Now imagine filling a tub with multiple faucets all turned on at the same time. The work of funding your budget is like filling a tub. Too often, we rely on one spigot rather than opening multiple pathways for people to express their generosity. How many opportunities do you provide for people to support your mission? Are all your efforts concentrated on the weekly offering, or are other options available and promoted? In **Worksheet 12**, list ways people give financially to your mission.

Kennon Callahan[2] suggests a mix of giving opportunities that supports the Multiple Spigots Theory. He recommends multiple offerings and invitations throughout the year (see **Figure 6**). Consider how these strategies complement one another and the number of times these opportunities are recommended.

---

2 Kennon Callahan, *Giving and Stewardship in an Effective Church* (San Francisco: HarperSanFrancisco, 1992), 49–59.

If conducted creatively and strategically, many faith communities could include a special or missional offering much more frequently.

Type of Gifts	Purpose Examples	Frequency
Weekly offerings	Operations/missions	52 times per year
Special offerings	Special needs (house fire, homeless)	3–6 per year
Missional offerings	Projects (Habitat, Heifer, UMCOR)	2–4 per year
Community worship experiences/offerings	Focus on the neighborhood, stranger, or newcomer in community	6 plus Christmas and Easter
Special projects giving/ capital campaigns	Address higher cost projects	Every 2–3 years

Figure 6

More Income Strategies

George Bullard's work, "A Baker's Dozen of Fundraising Streams," encourages expansion of revenue sources. His funding streams include tithes and offerings, designated offerings, capital funds campaigns, fees for events and services, product sales, fundraisers, planned gifts, investments, grants, partnerships and cooperatives, sale or lease of assets, community-oriented fundraisers, and building-use fees.[3] Many missions focus on only a few of these options. Let's take a closer look at some revenue-generating strategies.

Ask: Commitment or Pledge Invitation

Focusing on giving and generosity, including God's generosity, is the best way to generate funds for your mission goals. The most effective stewardship cultivation activity, making an ask, is also often the most challenging. Research confirms that pledged giving is three times unpledged giving.[4] Obstacles to

---

3 Rev. George Bullard, DMin, "A Baker's Dozen of Fundraising Streams," Columbia Area Metro Baptist Association, Copyright 2011. Used with permission.

4 Herb Miller, *New Consecration Sunday Stewardship Program* (Nashville, TN: Abingdon Press, 2002), 4–5, citing research by D. Hodge, C. Zech, P. McNamara, and M. Donahue, *Money Matters* (Louisville, KY: Westminster John Knox, 1996). Considered the workhorse of annual commitment campaigns, this model works multiple years and offers detailed instructions.

asking and other excuses like the challenges of fitting an annual commitment process into busy schedules limit our missional growth. Let's consider the reasons and resources for inviting commitments or pledges a bit more carefully.

The Pledge Drive: God Will Provide—or—Sign on the Dotted Line

Do you experience the annual giving campaign as a spiritual discipline? While some people may never complete a pledge card, many of us learn to express our trust in God's generosity by signing a commitment card or pledge form, demonstrating our giving intent. That intention often increases financial discipline and self-control, which can correlate with other blessings and accomplishments. Many curriculum resources are available, and each year, talented individuals create new liturgy to inspire generosity and giving commitments. While many pledge drives are short-term, offering occasional congregational studies that complement the commitment or stewardship ministry, even at a different time of year, engages more people in a variety of creative ways. While stewardship ministries are often held in the fall, consider other times of year. I have discovered that Advent, when we celebrate the gift of God's presence, is a great stewardship season. Contact your conference/judicatory offices or annual conference Foundation, or visit your denominational website to explore and find inspiration.

When considering the merits of conducting a commitment process each year, consider the following research. People asked to estimate their giving (i.e., use pledge or commitment cards) give twice as much as those who are not asked. People who don't experience an annual financial commitment campaign give an average of 1.5 percent of their income. People asked to consider percentage giving or tithing give, on average, 4.1 percent of their income. Asking for a written percentage-based goal or commitment triples the average gifts people offer.[5]

Remember:

- Giving is a practice and a habit; it requires practice. Encouragement helps too!

5 Miller, *New Consecration Sunday Stewardship Program*, 4–5.

- Words on paper are far more valuable than words spoken into the air.
- Annual financial goals strengthen both personal and missional stewardship.
- Annual commitment processes should encompass three to six weeks of inspiration and hope.
- Generosity is an action verb, not an adjective.

Don't Forget:

- People are smart and recognize begging, so keep your invitation . . . invitational.
- Laity testimonials may have more impact than sermons.
- Others are asking for support, and our missions miss their potential when we don't ask.
- New people come throughout the year; invite them to commit as part of their orientation to your mission. One study reports that for every month between becoming a member and being asked for a financial commitment, giving diminishes by 10 percent.
- Discipleship and membership are commitments; why delay bringing generosity to people's attention? If you aren't doing some sort of annual commitment activity, what is stopping you, and why are you accepting less support for your missions than research studies show is available?

Building-Use Agreements

Carefully negotiated written agreements between ministries, mission projects, community service agencies, and other partners can generate significant revenue for sites with underutilized property. Nonprofits need to partner with other nonprofits to protect their legal status, but a variety of missional or entrepreneurial enterprises are emerging and will generate more possibilities in the future. With increasing underutilized property, opportunities to expand mission activities as well as revenue should to continue to grow.

Capital Campaign

When significant infrastructure costs, deferred maintenance, or expansion projects reach 100 percent or more of the current operating budget amount, consider conducting a capital campaign. Campaigns typically run three to nine months with a pledge repayment time frame of one to three years. Successful capital campaigns typically generate from 1.5 to 3 times the annual budget and are typically effective every three to five years because new donors emerge. Debt-reduction campaigns typically generate only 1 to 1.5 times the annual budget and may need to be held multiple times to reduce the debt load some building projects incur. Consultants are highly recommended and increase campaign results due to higher accountability, coaching, and encouragement. Fees, if any, are a percentage of the campaign or preferably a set fee for the project.

Collections: Penny/Bottle Drive or Other Redemptions

Like crows, people collect things, especially shiny things! As environmental awareness and recycling industries grow, more opportunities for collecting, recycling, and redeeming products for cash incentives will emerge. Online businesses promoting recycling with cash rewards are likely to continue to create new opportunities. Microfinancing aspects of online shopping that triggers donations to charities is just one rapidly growing area. As long as people use stuff, entrepreneurs will seek partners in the collection and repurposing industry, and your mission can benefit.

Community Events/Meals

Feeding ministries and community meals are often part of missional fundraising. Coming together to cook, set up, serve, and clean up food for a donation or ticketed sales occurs monthly in some settings. Valuable fellowship and team-building also occur; however, burnout and dependence on increasingly smaller work teams can discourage volunteer resources. Assessing the costs associated with materials, unpaid labor, and time commitments to plan, shop, prepare, and market these meals may reveal that the costs in time and talent outweigh the revenue generated. However, these traditions have staying power, and new versions are likely to emerge.

Other events, such as concerts or other performances, craft fairs, or festivals also require large investments of time and talent to plan and execute, with a wide range of financial results. Community culture and missional identity also impact the revenue-generating results. With careful assessment of cost-benefit ratios, these events may continue to generate meaningful income.

Designated Giving Invitations

In a designated gifts campaign, donors adopt a specific project or mission expense. These short-term designations inspire giving for specific items such as a monthly oil bill, a snowplowing invoice, or Sunday school materials that appeal to donors' interest. One donor may find supporting a pension fund appealing while another may prefer underwriting adult study materials. Contributions may be honorary—for example, sponsoring a musical anthem or the altar flowers. One church's designated giving effort ANGELS (Answering the Need for Gifts of Extraordinary Love and Service) raised more than $4,000 in three months with sponsorships of newsletters, worship bulletins, or choir anthems. Designations allow donors to identify how their gift will benefit current expenses and are different from longer-term designated funds, such as the Memorial Fund. This strategy works for new or extraordinary needs unanticipated during the budget-setting process or to encourage stronger generosity.

Electronic Giving

As fewer people use paper checks, donors expect various forms of electronic giving options. Whether initiated through personal online banking or vendor-supported withdrawals, more revenue will be received on weekdays. Phone, text, and app-initiated payments will increase as emerging leaders adopt those platforms for their financial transactions. While setting up a kiosk in your mission space may feel uncomfortable, equipping donors to give in the manner they prefer will support your mission resourcing endeavors.

Grants

Foundations and local agencies may offer opportunities to apply for grant funding to support missional activities. Alignment with the funder's vision and purpose is important, and application processes range from simple to complex. While grant funding offers a healthy infusion of resources, these funding streams are seldom long-term, and applicants need to keep generating new ideas for projects that align with the funder's priorities while also working to replace grant funding in the long term. An experienced grant writer can generate quality proposals and raise significant dollars. When creating a grant proposal, carefully read the instructions to understand the grantor's wishes. The amount of time and energy invested in what are typically short-term funding opportunities should be weighed carefully against other opportunities and strategies that generate more sustainable income.

Special Offerings/5th Sunday/Second-Mile Giving

Because the most effective way to invite generosity and increase resources is to Ask For It—the AFI method—there are many creative ways to spark donor generosity. These include special designations for the four 5th-Sunday offerings each year or inviting people to go a second mile in their giving for a specific mission. Special offerings might recognize a special event, time, or accomplishment or an urgent need. Any variation of giving invitations is typically effective because people tend to be highly motivated by need or challenges. One small rural congregation I visited responded to the pastor's challenge to help a student enroll in driver's education by raising over $400 one Sunday.[6] Our fear of asking causes us to consistently underestimate the giving capacity of others, and our faith should embolden us to connect donors to missional needs much more frequently.

Tithing

The biblical discipline of tithing goes in and out of vogue as our culture continues to transform and be transformed. Despite the cultural vacillation, ask tithers; their responses will be that tithing works and creates a grateful heart. Tithing, a discipline that makes giving more intentional, simply works. Introduce tithing or growth in giving by inviting donors to practice tithing for one month or to give 10 percent of their tax refund or other bonuses to missions. These options invite percentage-based growth with a generosity step customized to the donor's personal financial situation.

Complete **Worksheet 13. Giving Opportunity Plan** to build a plan for

---

6 Pastor Mimi McGee, Cornerstone UMC, Saco, ME. Used with permission.

implementing additional missional invitations to reach donors and engage them as missional partners. With all these options to explore, I am always puzzled when a congregation's first response to financial challenges is so often to cut the budget. Motivating generosity requires engaging in multiple growth-oriented options before reducing our mission activities. Approaching finances with confidence and from a positive perspective, believing in God's possibilities, may be the most important income-generating, generosity-motivating shift for church leaders. These tests of faith call us to step up even when that means stepping in a new direction.

When Our Mission Requires More Resources

Concerns or questions about financial sustainability will arise at some point in time, and there will be prophecy about when funds will be gone. Despite these clarion calls for accountability, such predictions seldom come true. A surprise monetary gift occurs, or other options are explored and implemented, either delaying the forecasted deadlines or turning the mission focus in a new direction. However, even missional churches tend to be risk-averse and slow to change, sometimes missing new opportunities to fulfill their mission of sharing the love of Jesus. Before rushing to sell off assets or into desperate fundraising ideas, wise leaders first take an honest look at their ministry context and their impact on members and community.

As scripture says, when there is no vision, the people perish. Where there is no vision, no mission occurs. Financial challenges are always spiritual challenges. Here are a few provocative questions about mission and purpose. Studying these may be a better investment than another fundraiser if your resources are limited.

1. Do current members reside in the local community or only spend time in the area for worship or meetings?
2. Does the worshiping community reflect the neighborhood where it is located?
3. Do members actively participate in mission or service projects, or are contributions mostly financial?
4. Does your history include unresolved trauma or conflict?

5. Do the leaders focus on *the way we were* or on looking for new ministry opportunities?

Fuzzy purpose and identity, inward focus, unresolved conflict, and even population migration have a greater impact on your mission than any fund-raiser. Facing these challenges is hard, and reality checks may indicate significant culture shifts are needed. Why should members who define their church as *sanctuary*—where safety and stability are most important—ever really embrace the scriptural mandate to engage in constant and ongoing *transformation*? These two motivations are real and biblical and yet can pull us in opposite directions. Sanctuary and transformation is a polarity we need to manage, not attempt to fix or, worse, place in competition with each other. Engage a process consultant to guide a revisioning journey that increases honesty and accountability during a time of transformational change. When new life emerges, this hard work is rewarded.

Additional Campaign Options

Once again, the most effective option for securing additional resources continues to be the ask. Weekly giving invitations offered in an inspiring manner will generate results. In addition to the options described, a couple of other options merit consideration.

Miracle Sunday[7] is a campaign option that invites members to prayerfully consider a three- to six-week special appeal with a specific goal. The ask could be paying off a debt, funding a new mission, or stretching to meet an immediate need or goal. Miracle Sunday typically generates about 10 to 15 percent of your annual budget. Because there is little preparation or additional activity during the campaign, it relies on inspiring and clear communication about its purpose, hence the title Miracle Sunday. One long-tenured pastor, seeking to gift his successor with a balanced budget, needed to raise $30,000 in a few months: a perfect Miracle Sunday scenario. Initially, the pastor was uncomfortable asking anyone to support a campaign in honor of his

---

7 "Miracle Sunday: A Year's Income in a Day," in *The Abingdon Guide to Funding Ministry*, vol. 3 (Nashville, TN: Abingdon Press, 1997), 116–18. The series contains articles, resources, and tips for financial stewardship including worship resources, campaign models, communication, and best practices as well as legal information.

years of faithful service. When he was invited to consider that people would either give him mementos to carry around for the rest of his life, or he could direct their desire to express gratitude for his leadership toward his goal of a balanced budget, he decided on Miracle Sunday. By the time the pastor retired, the church successfully balanced its budget.[8] Everyone got what they wanted and needed, a miracle created by God's people.

While a leader needs to be discerning, even after multiple campaigns, if the need still exists, consider another campaign. Needs are seldom met without an ask of some kind. Develop a different invitation to create a new opportunity for donors. And, even if the last campaign was just three years ago, new people are ready for an invitation to support God's ministry. Campaigns are times to focus on others' generosity, not our own personal fatigue or limitations.

Ultimately, when unmet needs continue to exist, another stewardship commitment or pledge campaign is needed. Carefully communicating the consequences of allowing God's ministry to be underfunded will reveal new possibilities or confirm the need to consider other options for the future. Most donors hold back a bit of their giving capacity for a surprise challenge or need. Leaders need to courageously and clearly state what is needed and invite others to join them in responding. Leaders may no longer stay in their personal comfort zone and avoid challenging people. Until the leaders' and givers' hearts are joyfully transformed, we have not fully become God's stewards. Leaders don't do anyone any favors if they allow fiscal insolvency.

In some cases, we prevent others from exercising their generosity. We don't recognize offerings and end up creating barriers that limit our mission. During a campaign for a $50,000 garden in a memory-care facility, a group of leaders and donors gathered for a project update. While these donors would be approached individually later, each attendee was asked to make an initial $500 commitment. One attendee left abruptly. When asked to follow up with this donor, staff deferred, saying this gentleman was really busy and they didn't want to bother him. The error of that assumption became clear when he donated $400,000 to another local project shortly after that

---

8 Rev. Mark Demers, First United Methodist Church, Burlington, VT. Used with permission.

meeting. It is quite possible that we discount others' giving capacity through our assumptions.

Finally, remember an ask is a conversation with many possible responses. Donor priorities may align with an annual gift or with a planned gift or with a capital gift. Keep these conversations flexible so that any option that matches a donor's wishes remains possible. Donors give clear feedback about their readiness. When a young couple I visited during a capital campaign left their three-year-old twins alone at the dinner table to meet with me in the living room, I suggested it clearly wasn't a good time for this conversation and rescheduled. People are speaking; we just need to listen.

Planned Giving: Future Security Today

Can your generosity outlast you? Yes! Several types of gifts help donors support missions beyond their lifetime. Donors and our missions benefit from planned gifts, and leaders need basic planned-giving knowledge for large gifts. Planned gifts and endowments help donors and missions work together to create income for future generations. Some missions have received significant sustainable income due to visionary decisions made decades ago. Promoting planned giving and building endowments provides income stability for your mission.

"I wish my mom had known about planned gifts!" —a participant's comment after an introductory presentation to a women's group.

Planned gifts allow donors to express their generosity using accumulated assets. Donors or missions create endowments by making gifts oriented to the future. While an organization may create an endowment program before any gifts are received, a planned gift is an actual financial transaction. Through a planned gift, generous people share their assets and invest in your mission. Even people with limited resources can plan good gifts; planned gifts come in all sizes. Created during a person's lifetime, donors participate in the design and decision-making process. Planned gifts are created by bequests or by life-income options, such as charitable gift annuities or trusts, or by accumulated assets, such as stocks or property, which grow in value over time, and fund planned gifts, reinvesting assets in mission. Gifting accumulated assets benefits donors by avoiding some tax consequences and simplifying estate planning. Planned gifts may also fund current or new endowments. Coaching by a financial planner or attorney facilitates the creation of a gift plan that maximizes benefits for the donor and the recipient.

Planned-giving education and testimonials inspire donors by demonstrating creative ways to participate in God's plan and vision for the world. Creating an Endowment or Stewardship Committee to educate members about planned gifts encourages these future-oriented gifts. Since planned gifts are often bequests, helping people create their estate plans or review their wills continues to be an effective planned-giving activity. Accurate documentation that protects bequests, memorial gifts, and planned gifts should be maintained by any entity aware of such gifts. See **Worksheet 14. Gift Record Tracking Template** for help in safeguarding accurate documentation.

Endowments

Endowments receive gifts expected to exist permanently; *endow* means to provide a source of income. If a gift is endowed, the donor's intent is to preserve the original amount or *principle* of the gift in perpetuity. Endowment policies describe the methods and procedures for managing planned or endowed gifts. Endowed gifts are intended to provide future benefits, that is, income! Endowments may receive planned and ordinary gifts. Many missions create an organized endowment program to recognize and encourage gifts from supporters' assets or estates. The organization defines the categories in which gifts are designated, determines whether proposed gifts are appropriate, and decides how funds are invested, managed, and publicized and how supporters are educated. For example, an endowed Music Fund could distribute income after the fund reached a principal balance of $1,000. Because endowment funds are typically invested, their financial growth is expected to exceed returns from bank accounts.

Learn the different ways your mission receives gifts and communicate as many options as possible for donors. This may require some new skills. How silly it would be to reject a gift of stock during an annual campaign because we aren't sure how to receive it. Yet it happens. **Worksheet 15. Fundraising Quiz** tests your knowledge about options for expanding income for your missions. Good luck!

Reflection Questions

1. How do you feel about talking about generating income or fundraising to support your mission?
2. Could you respond more than three to six times a year to extraordinary needs?
3. If Jesus asked for financial support for missions that change the world, how do you think people would respond?
4. Describe the most inspiring mission fundraising effort you supported. Why did it inspire you?
5. When was your last capital campaign, and how do people remember it?
6. Select three strategies from the chapter and explore why and how your mission will implement or strengthen them.

CHAPTER SIX

EXPENDITURES

Distributing the Gifts

I can't be on your finance committee; you get ministry done with, what looks like on paper, clearly insufficient resources.

—Abraham Waya[1]

When we complain about not having enough
we inevitably do it with our mouths full.

—Steve Garnaas-Holmes

Our financial systems for distributing the gifts we steward are as important as our systems for discipling members and, likewise, will encourage or discourage generosity. If doubts exist in our membership or in our community about financial accountability, integrity, or financial transparency, our efforts will suffer, and our mission will fail. As financial stewardship becomes increasingly complex and technology-dependent—making some tasks easier—our systems, training, and resources for sound financial management will evolve. Whether you are still using ledgers or have invested in high-tech software, the purpose of your financial system is

1 Rationale given by a certified public account declining to serve on a local church finance committee; shared by Rev. Dr. Abraham Waya, Central United Methodist Church, Brockton, MA. Used with permission.

responsible stewardship and fiscal accountability. Let's explore some foundational components of managing how we distribute funds.

Authorization

Once officially adopted by the governing body, the expense budget establishes amounts authorized for expenditures, thereby authorizing the treasurer to pay expenses up to the approved amounts for bills and obligations. When expenses exceed available funds, the treasurer notifies the finance leadership and, if needed, the governing body of your church. Significant budget changes may warrant calling a special board meeting known in The United Methodist Church as a Charge Conference. If your financial stewardship practices do not follow this governance format, a review of roles and responsibilities may be needed. Nonprofit organizations are governed by an elected board that approves fund distribution by adopting an expense authorizing budget. That authority is not delegated to any other groups or individuals. How does your financial system and management work?

Cash-Flow Cushion or Reserves

Because actual income and expenses will not align exactly with budget plans, funds available in bank accounts, also known as balances, will fluctuate. Treasurers and finance leadership manage *cash flow* by monitoring income and expenses' impact on bank account balances so that resources are available when bills need to be paid. Treasurers may face difficult choices about what to pay, and delays in paying bills may create an illusion of surplus funds. Sluggish income or gifts given on an annual basis create a perception of insufficient funds. One option for managing cash flow is identifying an amount of cash as reserves—or *cushion*—drawn upon when needed and replenished when possible. This float activity should be explained during a budget presentation, and will appear clearly during an audit or financial review. Careful attention ensures cash-flow reserves remain available or are replenished promptly. Proper accounting practices strongly discourage maintaining cash-flow reserves by borrowing from designated funds. This practice causes great stress for treasurers and erodes trust and confidence in financial management and stability. Finance leaders need full disclosure of all bank account balances to manage cash flow and build donor confidence. With many churches living with tight budgets, maintaining any reserves may be a challenging yet valuable stewardship goal.

Managing cash flow requires awareness of trends in both income and expenses. Consider these trends, which impact cash flow needs:

- Giving and income is often greatest in the month of December.
- Summer months are lean in some areas; in others they are the busiest.
- Expenses increase in some areas in the winter, for snow removal and heating costs, while other areas face greater energy costs during the summer because of air-conditioning.
- Infrastructure costs, such as utilities, insurance, and trash disposal costs, typically increase even if your mission isn't growing.

A positive bank balance or *cushion* maintained in a bank account or set aside in a reserve account equips treasurers to manage cash flow. A positive bank balance or *cushion* allows a treasurer to pay a $10,000 plowing bill in January before the actual income for this expense is received in that calendar year. Cash flow allows a mission trip deposit to be paid before all the fundraising is done. Reserve funds for managing cash flow are a healthy stewardship and stress-reducing discipline.

Prayer Pause: How much reserve funding is enough for your ministry?

Depending on economic conditions, *cushion* amounts may range from one to six months of expenses, typically two to three months. Congregations have different expectations, comfort levels, and capacity. One congregation will be relieved to have $25 in the bank after paying bills, another may panic when the bank balance falls below $25,000. Learn your leaders' comfort level and *cushion* expectations. One congregation announced a financial crisis with a bank balance of over $25,000 and $15,000 in memorial funds. Listening more closely, I discovered that this was their cash-flow reserve and appropriate for the size of their ministry. We worked on investing the memorial funds in ministry and communicating more carefully the purpose of these reserves. There are stories behind those needs and preferences that wise leaders need to understand.

Asking *How much is enough?* will generate as many different answers as *What is your favorite travel destination?* Answers depend on past experiences, current hopes, and overall confidence. It may be healthier to grow reserves or to reduce them. The conversation about financial expectations is a more important stewardship exercise than any answer the conversation may generate. The unhealthiest response is silence and avoidance. Too many missions persist in completely avoiding this conversation. When honest talk occurs, personal wisdom, historical baggage, or, sometimes, unhealed trauma is unearthed. Delving into our personal and congregational hopes and expectations for financial stewardship deserves our time, attention, and, at times, pastoral care.

Categories of Expenses

Not all expenses have the same types of consequences, hence some appear to have varying degrees of importance. Some expenses are *fixed*, while others are *variable*, which may or may not accurately reflect their importance. An electric bill may cause immediate consequences when unpaid; the cost of not paying paper supply invoices may undermine community relationships. Personnel and property costs are considered fixed costs. Other variable costs, such as program supplies, which could be purchased or donated by supporters, are often the first hit in a challenging budget-setting environment. If your treasurer is struggling to pay bills, reread the previous chapter and evaluate communication so that generosity is built and hope is voiced.

Rediscovering a new missional purpose in your community is hard work; however, God's plan has certainly not been fulfilled and your next vision may be knocking on your door. Rather than asking if anyone would notice if you were gone, consider the possibility that God has already planted a new vision and purpose; the challenge is simply to see it. Every expenditure of resources is an act of trust in the unknown future, an investment in the communities that support us, even if they never step on our property. Shifting our mind-set to see expenditures as an investment in missions and in our communities will take work, but it will change everything about managing expenses. Rather than an obligation, we become investors and cocreators with God, even if we are still not sure what is being planted.

Consequences of Budget Cuts

Monitoring expenditures eventually triggers a protective reflex to reduce expenditures. Some missions need greater accountability, and change can offer cost-saving opportunities. Leaders also need to carefully consider whether the urge to reduce costs is anxiety-driven or ministry-driven. Jumping to budget reductions before fully exploring capacity for growth will drive some potential resources away and accelerate a downward missional spiral. Churches tend to underestimate their capacity—and God's plans. With charitable giving continuing to increase and average giving rates stuck way below the biblical tithe, clear opportunities for growth exist in most situations.

When budget reductions become impossible to avoid, cuts typically occur in program areas or in staff support. Research through the study "A Strategic Plan for Growth in The United Methodist Church" indicates these two categories are the most highly correlated to church growth.[2] Cuts in these areas are more likely to accelerate decline than to slow it down. Many churches inadvertently accelerate their shortage of resources as they attempt to protect their ministry through budget cuts (see **Worksheet 16. Budget Balancing Options**).

Consider carefully the unintended consequences of budget reductions. Another option to consider is creating a tiered budget that identifies essential funding needs, missional funding needs, and funding visions. In some cases, when the vision has turned completely inward or the capacity to serve others has eroded beyond recovery, distributing resources to another ministry may be a legacy option worth considering. However, simply categorizing struggling missions as legacy or hospice ministries may also inadvertently accelerate decline. Seek guidance from denominational leaders and congregational development and stewardship practitioners to navigate these difficult but also life-giving conversations.

---

2 Donald R. House Sr., "A Strategic Plan for Growth in The United Methodist Church" (Institute for Local Church Growth: September 2015), 12–21.

Investing in new possibilities is an alternative to managing decline. Rather than focusing on cuts, consider taking steps to improve the excellence of your mission work, especially adult programs, so that new awareness of the mission and its impact encourages giving to fund the missions and potentially resume positive growth. Discover stewardship growth opportunities using **Worksheet 17. Stewardship Assessment**. Consider investing in some of these practices for encouraging generosity and cultivating resources for mission work.

Expense Overages

The approved budget estimates anticipated expenses and determines the amounts the treasurer can pay for expenses when they occur. A treasurer cannot change the expense budget approved by the governing body even though expenses may vary or be unpredictable. Financial reports track actual payments against budget amounts to monitor remaining funds available. When expenses or unpaid invoices exceed the approved budget amounts, consultation with the finance leadership and governing body is needed. Treasurers report spending overages and may have suggestions for budget adjustments, but the Finance Committee and Church Council reviews and approves changes. One option for creating some budget flexibility is to adopt a threshold—for example, allowing expenses to exceed the budget by 5 or 10 percent—if the bottom line doesn't change, before action by the council is needed. Clarity about procedures and expectations will increase transparency and trust and promote generosity.

Invoices

Treasurers pay bills based on statements from vendors providing services or products. The receipt or vender invoice identifies the expenditure, when the purchase was made, the amount, and the vendor's name and contact information. Accounting best practices strongly discourage making payments without receipts or some form of documentation. In addition, payment of ministry expenses should be made directly to vendors rather than reimbursing members for expenditures they incur for mission activities. Avoid mingling organizational finances and personal finances. Processing payments by verbal or informal communication is also strongly discouraged because that can lead to problems in the audit review and financial integrity. Documentation, such as handwritten notes, are better than no documentation, although not ideal. Leaders and staff processing financial invoices should initial or sign the vender invoice, note the date approved, and assign the bill to a budget category or line item.

A simple requisition or request-for-payment form provides additional documentation and security for your financial management (see **Figure 7**). The vendor invoice—receipt or bill—is attached to the requisition form for recordkeeping. A requisition form provides checks and balances and simplifies the treasurer's work by streamlining information. The requisition form identifies who will be paid, what the payment is for, the amount and account to charge, and the signature of the person authorized to approve payment by the treasurer. This form also reminds leaders if there is a policy requiring more than one authorizing signature for expenses greater than, for example, $500 or $1,000. When electronic payments are made, confirmation documents should be printed and saved to verify payment and for audit review.

REQUISITION FORM SAMPLE

Work Area ______________ Date Requested ______________

Pay to the Order of ______________ Vendor Name ______________

Amount Requested ______________ Vendor Contact ______________

Vendor Phone ______________

Address ______________________________

Purpose ______________________________

Dept. Signature ______________________________

Mission Acct. Number ______________________________

Second Approval ______________________________

Instructions: Please attach receipts, packing slips, and invoices if applicable. If a bill or invoice is attached, the address can be left blank. If the check is to be made out to a company, please include a contact name. Approval is required to authorize an expense reimbursement to a staff member.

Office Use Only:

Check Number __________ Online Banking Confirmation ______________

Figure 7. Requisition Form Sample

Why is this documentation important? Leaders need to avoid placing staff at risk for unauthorized expenditures. It is tempting to spend others' money when signature policies are lax. Shortly after completing an interim director position, I received a call from the new director asking if I had authorized the purchase of a new laptop computer for the office. We discovered the former office manager had signed up for a credit card in the name of the agency and then used it to purchase a laptop. Are you vulnerable to this sort of misconduct? What steps are needed to prevent this risk?

Recordkeeping

The financial recordkeeping system, usually managed by the treasurer and perhaps a bookkeeper and office administrator, tracks the budget in categories that equip the finance leadership to monitor the budget, income, expenses, and cash flow. The actual line items in the system may be more detailed than the adopted budget and need to be specific enough to indicate where expenses should be charged. Exceedingly complex charts of accounts may be desired by treasurers but may be overwhelming to finance leaders. Determine the level of accounting detail needed for your mission.

Software packages for financial management exist with varying prices and degrees of user friendliness. Some integrate membership, program registration, payroll, and electronic giving features, which typically increase costs. While an electronic spreadsheet (such as Excel) is better than a paper ledger, it may still fall short of your needs. Every electronic system and software program will need some level of adaptation and take time to learn and set up. Careful consideration of user friendliness, volunteer and staff skills, as well as cost is encouraged. Investing in training to support staff and volunteers who use these software packages maximizes their usefulness. While the goal of technology is to save time, electronic financial systems also require a commitment of time and regular use to fully benefit from such resources.

All systems should be backed up with data saved in at least one additional location. In the event of total loss of financial records, use banking institutions' records to rebuild your system. What will you do if your financial information is lost or destroyed? Do you have a backup plan?

Reflection Questions

1. After reading this chapter, do you feel comfortable or uncomfortable about how your ministry stewards, handles, and distributes funds for mission activities and related costs?
2. How does financial management knowledge impact your generosity, your trust, and your confidence in your ministry's stewardship?
3. What ideas, suggestions, or questions do you have for your church and its leadership?
4. Is the way financial gifts are shared in your mission more like Martha, who focused on getting the work done, or like Mary, who poured precious oils on Jesus's feet?
5. After taking a careful look at your accounting procedures and systems, what tools do you need? What, if anything, needs to be replaced? What training would you recommend to your staff, whether paid or volunteer?

CHAPTER SEVEN

LEADERSHIP

People Who Count

Tell me, what is it you plan to do
with your one wild and precious life?

—Mary Oliver[1]

Leaders include people and groups who assume responsibilities, tend to tasks, point us toward new visions, and hold us accountable. Leaders help us to remember our purpose, call, and mission commitments to discipling others' leadership development, which can sometimes get lost in the ordinary tasks of ministry. Even the early disciples responded to the needs of others by organizing systems to deploy leadership (see Acts 6:1-6). Individuals who serve as stewards, counters, committee members, treasurers, financial secretaries, pastors, project or event leaders, and any activity involving the collection, management, or stewardship of money deserve our best support and protection.[2] Pastors may delegate financial responsibilities to laity, but they should not abdicate these responsibilities. A basic understanding of financial concepts is necessary for leaders today, both lay and clergy.

1 Mary Oliver, "The Summer Day," in *House of Light* (Boston, MA: Beacon Press, 1990), 60.

2 Additional resources for job descriptions and responsibilities are available through denominational resources such as the Guidelines Series, www.umcdiscipleship.org/leadership-resources/ministry-guidelines, and Discipleship Ministries, www.umcdiscipleship.org.

The gifts of laypersons' spiritual and practical skills, ranging from professional accounting and ease working with numbers to asking insightful questions, deserves our appreciation and professional support. In addition, insurance coverage should include a form of bonding and professional liability protection for church financial officers and volunteers, including the pastor. Some of these dedicated individuals plan their lives around when the offering needs to be counted, including Christmas Eve and other holidays, or when reports need to be generated. Clergy and the financial officers need to review the expectations and burdens placed on these persons.

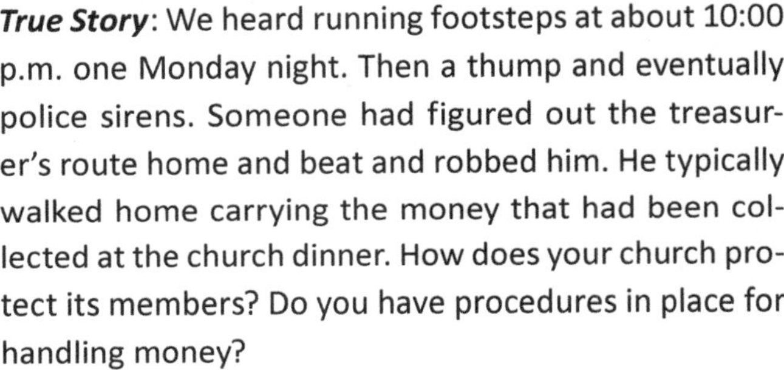

True Story: We heard running footsteps at about 10:00 p.m. one Monday night. Then a thump and eventually police sirens. Someone had figured out the treasurer's route home and beat and robbed him. He typically walked home carrying the money that had been collected at the church dinner. How does your church protect its members? Do you have procedures in place for handling money?

More Is Less . . . Risky

Some believe minimizing the number of people involved in financial management is a best practice, assuming that fewer people involved in this work reduces risk. Increasingly, however, best practices encourage *multiple eyes* and *safety in numbers*. More involvement generates more safety for all and healthier stewardship. Safe Sanctuary policies for abuse prevention protect adults *and* children from harm by preventing adults from being left alone with children. Similarly, the best financial practice is that no one is ever alone with money as it moves from donors' hands to the bank. The following persons all have contact with gifts and deserve protection as they serve in these roles.

Counters

Counters work in teams of at least two unrelated persons who do not live in the same household. They count and record gifts immediately following an event or at the end of a worship service so that funds are moved to the bank as soon as possible. To assess the safety of these persons and their financial role, consider the following questions:

- Are the counters always at least two unrelated persons not living in the same household?
- Are counters trained and supplied with resources, documents, and tools for this task?
- Are offerings counted and deposited in a bank within twenty-four hours?
- Are reports or documentation delivered to the financial secretary and treasurer for recording?
- How are gifts received during the week held before counting?

This review protects people like Charles. Charles counted the thrift store income by himself and earned the highest level of trust and accountability with his detailed reports. However, when $400 went missing, he had no protection. He and other leaders walked on eggshells for years. Eventually, the funds were found in one of the special event cash boxes. A simple human error damaged relationships and destroyed trust for years, and it could have all been avoided. If any of your volunteers are counting money alone, leadership must intervene and ensure their safety by creating counting teams.

Prayer Pause: Would your pastor be supported if she or he discovered a risky situation and needed to confront a long-term member to increase safety?

Financial Secretary

Income recordkeeping by a financial secretary, an elected officer, includes recording pledges, financial commitments, tracking gifts by family or giving unit, and recording all sources of income. The financial secretary sends reports to donors and to the finance leadership. A financial procedures review during your annual audit includes these questions:

- Are donor records updated annually, including pledge or commitment amounts?

- Are all gifts and payments by donors recorded by the financial secretary in a timely manner, including designated gifts, such as event registrations or memorial gifts?
- Are statements sent to donors according to legal requirements annually and quarterly for donor cultivation?

All financial contributions by donors are recorded by the financial secretary to generate an accurate end-of-year giving statement provided to each identified donor. Weekly giving envelopes facilitate this gift tracking process. Designated gifts for specific events or activities such as retreat registration or memorials, even if transferred to the trustees or distributed to another entity, are recorded by the financial secretary. Donors deserve a full and accurate summary of their annual contributions for tax purposes and accountability that cultivates generosity (see **Figure 8**).

When a donor receives a tangible benefit or items from a contribution, the contribution isn't fully qualified as a tax deduction. Donors' giving records report undesignated or pledge contributions separately from designated gifts, such as a capital campaign gift, and separately from gifts where a tangible benefit was received by the donor, such as a seat at a fundraising dinner where the donor receives a meal. Other donations may be tax deductible and need an appropriate gift acknowledgment letter.

[Mission Name and Address]	
Name ______________________________ Address ____________________________	
Date ________________	
Pledge Amount	
Pledge Payments to Date	$ __________
Other Contributions	$ __________
Payments (Not Tax-Deductible)	$ __________
Total to Date	$ __________
Excluding contributions listed as payments, no gifts or services were received as result of these contributions.	

Figure 8: Financial Giving Statement Sample

Pastor

As the spiritual and temporal leader of a faith community and mission site, pastors have oversight responsibilities; however, they should recuse themselves from financial transactions. Are these statements true about you as a pastor or of your expectations of your pastor?

- Pastors should not be signers on church accounts.
- Pastors should know the budget and financial procedures, and should participate in financial oversight and review. United Methodist pastors are also identified as administrative officers.[3]
- Pastors steward giving information in ways that build trust and generosity. The pastor has responsibility for stewarding donor information to ensure compliance with tax regulations and for pastoral care.[4]

Take a moment to reflect on the current and emerging expectations about the role of the pastor. Is the pastor a mission champion, coach, leader, manager, spiritual director, lead donor, steward, preacher, friend, or all of the above? With these diverse expectations, pastors must negotiate these roles with each faith community. Pastoral interest in teaching giving and stewardship principles as part of discipleship training influences the giving practices of donors and the funds raised to support church mission. This is not good news for a pastor hoping to delegate financial responsibilities to laity and avoid dealing with numbers and money. **Worksheet 18. Pastoral Role Expectations** invites leaders and pastors to reflect on their current expectations and stewardship communications in your ministry setting.

Whether pastors should have knowledge of donor giving has been thoroughly debated; stewardship practitioners urge disclosure, while many laity still prefer confidentiality. Stewarding donor information is a responsibility assigned to United Methodist pastors by the *Book of Discipline* in the denominational by-laws (see **Worksheet 19. Pastoral Stewardship of Giving**

3 "Responsibilities and Duties of Elders and Licensed Pastors," in *The Book of Discipline of The United Methodist Church: 2016* (Nashville, TN: Abingdon Press, 2016), ¶340.2c(1); "The Charge Conference," in *The Discipline*, ¶244.3.

4 "Responsibilities and Duties of Elders and Licensed Pastors," in *The Discipline*, ¶340.2c(2)(c).

Records). Ultimately, if we can't trust our pastors with our financial information, we shouldn't trust them with any of our personal information. And if we are comfortable with our relationship with money and our response to God's generosity, it really doesn't matter who knows! Pastors and laity hold a wide range of expectations about the pastoral role in congregational finances, especially regarding giving information. Differing views develop over time based on personal and congregational values, history, and experience. The expectation of privacy about our giving impedes pastoral care and does not encourage generosity.

Some pastors talk openly about their responsibility as lead stewards; others need to challenge themselves or the faith community's norms. The conversation about pastoral knowledge of giving information is essential to build trust and integrity in financial stewardship.

> 2016 *UMC Book of Discipline* ¶340.2(c)(2)(c) describes professional pastoral responsibilities:
>
> "To provide leadership for the funding ministry of the congregation. To ensure membership care including compliance with charitable giving documentation requirements and to provide appropriate pastoral care, the pastor, in cooperation with the financial secretary, shall have access to and responsibility for professional stewardship of congregational giving records."

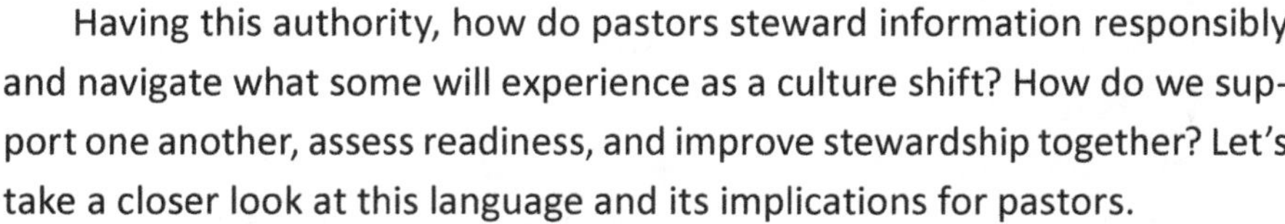

Having this authority, how do pastors steward information responsibly and navigate what some will experience as a culture shift? How do we support one another, assess readiness, and improve stewardship together? Let's take a closer look at this language and its implications for pastors.

Leadership

The first sentence articulates the responsibility to provide leadership for funding congregational ministry.

- Is a pastor expected to show up at every fundraising event or lead the annual pledge campaign?

- Do pastors direct the trustees' stewardship of assets or conduct all donor visits for capital campaigns?
- Is the pastor expected to calculate how much members should give or tithe, or is the pastor responsible for balancing the budget for the congregation?
- Does this language excuse laity from their responsibility for the financial health of their congregation?

No! None of these examples are recommended by stewardship practitioners; they are unrealistic and unhealthy. However, *leadership* clearly indicates a role for pastors. Faith communities and pastors must negotiate expectations and leadership norms to create contextual strategies for ensuring funding success for their ministry. In other words, each congregation and pastor must determine how leadership for funding their mission occurs. At the same time, financial stability will most likely require leadership.

Responsibility

Stewardship of giving information is a pastoral responsibility shared with the elected financial secretary. Despite the courageous leadership of stewardship educators challenging pastors to stop guessing donor capacity, some people still debate whether pastors knowing giving information is a healthy spiritual practice. This debate confirms how well we avoid what scares us. Deliberate reflection on the role of pastor as lead steward confirms that equipping pastors with factual data greatly improves their ability to grow the mission and provide pastoral care to all persons. Inspiring testimonials about transformational change due to donor information are growing as we reclaim Wesley's understanding of our relationship with money. It is a vital component of our spiritual formation. The resistance we encounter from both laity and clergy confirms the importance of this challenging spiritual task of a steward.

Laity as well as pastors desire success in faithful, joyful generosity. During different life stages, our capacity to express our generosity through financial gifts fluctuates. That reality is one of the key reasons pastors need to set aside fears and act as stewards. Stewardship advocates urge pastors to stop guessing how their members are expressing their gratitude to

God. Stewardship expert Clif Christopher suggests in a classic illustration that it is ridiculous to ask a medical doctor to diagnose an illness simply by looking at the patient. While a successful diagnosis is possible, it is much more likely if the doctor has more information. We must recognize giving as a spiritual act and a symptom of the health of our financial stewardship disciplines.

The voices that protest this level of pastoral leadership are often not comfortable with their own giving. Concerns about trust or pastoral care capabilities may trigger anxiety, so protecting others' feelings is one way to avoid the authentic self-searching that stewardship requires of us. We rationalize and make excuses to justify our giving limits and, consequently, often miss the rewards of joyful generosity. Fortunately, some pastors have claimed this pastoral leadership responsibility with positive impact on their mission capacity. Growth in generosity and giving is a predictable outcome of responsible knowledge about giving behaviors. Consider these testimonials about how giving knowledge impacts pastoral leadership:

- The eulogy I offered for a parishioner who consistently supported our children's ministry was a much stronger affirmation of his leadership and service than it would have been if I hadn't known of his designated gifts.
- When I was able to ask a leading family why their giving changed, I discovered their business had folded, and they were in crisis. What a blessing to be able to provide pastoral care during this challenging time in their lives.
- I realized I reduced my giving six months before I was consciously aware that I was heading into a divorce. My subconscious was taking protective measures that I only later understood.
- I knew the elderly gentleman who outlived his family members and continued to give to the church. I should have had a conversation with him about a legacy gift.

As pastors explore the implications of this responsibility in their ministry context, the vision of joyful generosity and more impactful pastoral care becomes a reality.

Treasurer

Another elected officer, the treasurer, is responsible for managing all financial transactions according to the adopted budget and providing reports and accounting functions, such as tax filings and financial status reports to finance leadership. While treasurers should not be involved in the counting or income processing, income activity appears in their reports. They are responsible for all payments and fund distributions. The following questions explore ways to support the treasurer:

- Is the treasurer given access to training and support for this important and time-consuming role?
- Are backup systems in place should the treasurer become incapacitated or have extended travel plans?
- Are payments limited to the approved budget and reviewed when beyond approved budget?
- Are payments accompanied by receipts and authorizing signature and invoice form?

Since The United Methodist Church allows congregations to compensate the financial secretary, treasurer, or business administrator, staffing options exist. Outsourcing this work or hiring bookkeepers whose work is supervised by the financial secretary and treasurer are other options. As volunteer resources shrink and the complexity of this work increases, we need creative options for managing this work efficiently.

Ushers

Ranging from small groups to teams with diverse ranges of ages, gender, and leadership experience, ushers transfer financial gifts from donors' hands, pockets, or wallets into containers used to collect these gifts. This is commonly referred to as *passing the plate* or *taking the collection*. In the future, look for increasingly creative offering rituals and practices that honor giver generosity. Changes in collection practices or the counting location should be carefully supervised. One church I visited left the money in the offering plates on a bench, in the hallway, during the fellowship time! To assess the ushers' safety and protect the gifts they collect, consider the following questions:

- Are gifts placed in the plate before the service and left unsupervised?
- Are the plates left in public view after the offering is collected?
- Are the ushers the same people each week or a rotating group of persons?
- Are the ushers trained, thanked, and coached on safety procedures?
- Who is responsible for moving the offering funds from the place of worship to the counting location?

Leadership Teams

Leaders also work with a variety of groups with different roles and responsibilities for financial stewardship in the missional church. The *Book of Discipline* and other denominational resources detail the responsibilities and structure of the teams mentioned below.

Church Council and Emerging Models

The governing body in a United Methodist church is the Charge Conference, meeting at least annually for salary approval, budget adoption, and other official business of the church. Between Charge Conferences, the governing authority is delegated to the Church Council, known in some settings as the Administrative Board or Council. Churches have flexibility in programmatic structure but are required to have administrative committees. Additional experimentation with smaller councils or leadership teams functioning as a "committee of the whole" continue to emerge as smaller groups seek to manage missions efficiently and effectively. Keeping stewardship a priority as churches explore different leadership models supports missional vision and service to the community.

Endowment Committee

In 1988, The United Methodist Church recognized planned giving as an important stewardship activity by enacting legislation for Permanent Endowment and Planned Giving Ministry Committees in every United Methodist church.[5] While not required, this ministry contributes to the financial sustainability of your mission. An Endowment Committee stewards assets and

5 "Permanent Endowment and Planned Giving Ministry Committee," in *The Discipline*, ¶2534.

endowment funds. Once established by action of the governing body, the Charge Conference, Endowment Committees organize, orient, and plan the marketing strategies for the endowment, working collaboratively with trustees and finance leadership. Responsibilities include managing endowments, invested funds, or major gifts, and educating donors about planned gifts and major gifts opportunities. Ongoing communication raises awareness and supports corporate memory of the vision and purpose of the endowment. See **Appendix C** for additional information and resources for developing an endowment program for your mission.

Finance Committee

Responsible for the stewardship and supervision of financial aspects of church mission, a United Methodist church's Finance Committee job description is outlined in the *Book of Discipline*. Responsibilities include raising funds to meet the adopted budget, supervision of financial procedures and management, supporting the treasurer and financial secretary, and reviewing and distributing reports and financial communications. Finance Committees often prioritize conserving, controlling, and constraining the use of financial resources and assets. These priorities may conflict with a Stewardship Committee's focus on experimentation, vision, and initiatives, which finance leaders may find risky. Having different groups responsible for finance and stewardship or fundraising activities is strongly recommended.

Mission Committee

While mission work is the responsibility of the whole faith community, the Mission Committee advocates for mission priorities and seeks opportunities to serve the community. These leaders coordinate, plan, and implement projects connecting resources and talents of the mission with local, regional, or international partners to share the love of Jesus with others through service, compassion, and resources. Some Mission Committees receive financial support in the annual budget while others conduct fundraising for selected projects. It is best to foster a collaborative relationship between mission leaders and finance leaders.

Stewardship Committee

The Stewardship Committee focuses on appreciation for God's generous abundance, on our personal management of God's gifts entrusted to us—time, talent, and resources—and how we use God's resources to care for others. Stewardship leaders often take responsibility for the annual financial appeal or pledge campaign. Since the Stewardship Committee's role extends beyond financial stewardship, persons with interests in environmental stewardship and outreach ministries also contribute to the work of stewardship leaders. Some Stewardship Committees also take on the role of education, communication, and talent inventories for current and new members. Matching personal gifts and talents, including skills and interests with ministry activities, is one way congregational stewardship supports leadership development.

The mind-set required for stewardship work is significantly different from financial management. **Figure 9** explores some of the differences between a financial mind-set and a stewardship or development mind-set, and the differing responsibilities. Consider the challenges this creates for finance leaders trying to do stewardship work.

Finance Mind-Set	**Stewardship Mind-Set**
Accountability	Generosity
Don't be too optimistic	Enthusiasm and high risk tolerance
Be conservative	Inspire and raise the bar
Focus on numbers and bottom line	Focus on people and gifts
People can be unreliable	Everything we need will be provided
Don't bite off more than you can chew	Big, audacious goals
Financial Responsibilities	**Stewardship Responsibilities**
Budget/planning/review	Year-round communicating/marketing
Systems/purchases/expenditures	Inspiring and affirming generosity
Audit/accountability	Teaching lifelong giving/planned giving
Policies/procedures	Cultivating donors

Figure 9

The larger the group of leaders supporting stewardship principles and activities, the greater the impact and infusion of stewardship throughout the mission. By keeping the focus on God's abundance and our invitation to be stewards on God's behalf, we become partners with God as well as resource developers and fundraisers.

Trustees

The biblical model of *stewards*, people who manage other people's property, continues today through our trustees who tend to the physical, maintenance, access, and furnishings needs of our houses of worship and other property. Trustees need enough resources to ensure the facilities and structures are safe and complement the mission.

In addition to property management responsibilities, trustees or any other body authorized by Charge Conference, such as an Endowment Committee, are responsible for reviewing and recommending acceptance, rejection, or renegotiation of bequests and capital gifts offered by donors. Trustees review donor restrictions, assess gift appropriateness, and may invite donors to expand restrictions before acceptance. For example, a gift restricted to building a handicap ramp could be expanded more broadly to all handicap accessibility needs. Recommendations to accept or reject a gift are reviewed by the Church Council/Board and accepted at an annual meeting or Charge Conference.

Trustees are elected by the governing board and assigned a term of office. They select their chairperson. The group works collaboratively with those responsible for staff (PPRC/SPRC[6]) when hiring personnel for property management. While the trustees negotiate with contractors and solicit bids for work, final approval for work should either be preapproved for a set dollar amount by budget action or require action by the governing body for approval. As trustees frequently engage professionals within the community, the church must pay careful attention to conflicts of interest. Trustees should disclose any family or business relationships with potential contractors or employees, and where there is such a relationship, recuse themselves from participating in action impacting work authorization.

In United Methodism, a *trust clause* ensures property is held in trust by the denomination. Faith communities purchase and use their property

6 Pastor/Parish Relations Committee (PPRC); Staff/Parish Relations Committee (SPRC).

including caring for management and maintenance, but the property may not be sold, demolished, or withdrawn from the denomination by local trustees. To protect the interests of future generations, a District Committee on Buildings and Church Location reviews property projects.

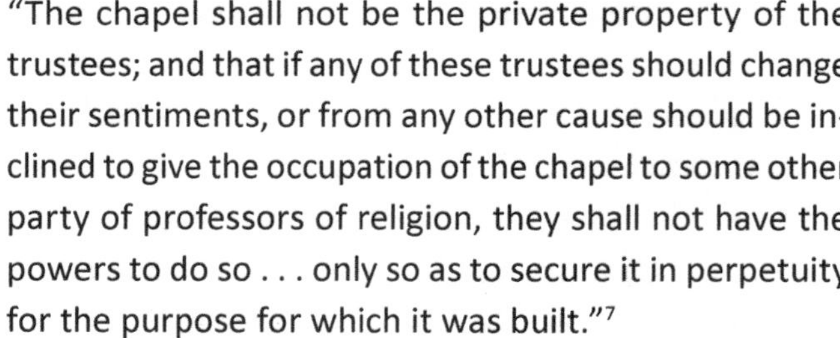

> "The chapel shall not be the private property of the trustees; and that if any of these trustees should change their sentiments, or from any other cause should be inclined to give the occupation of the chapel to some other party of professors of religion, they shall not have the powers to do so . . . only so as to secure it in perpetuity for the purpose for which it was built."[7]

The annual budget should include funds for the trustees' responsibilities. Some faith communities separate trustee funds from operating funds. While intending to protect funds for property and maintenance purposes, the practice of separate books and accounts may also lead to conflict, paternalistic relationships, and confusion. Nonprofit organizations account annually for all funds they receive or steward. All funds, unless stipulated by a will or planned giving document, fall under the supervision of the governing body: Church Council or Charge Conference. If trustee funds are separate from the general operating expenses, their spending plan and budget should be approved at Charge Conference. Trustee income and expenses need to be included in financial reports and are always included in the audit review. Some trustees elect a treasurer, who must be a member of the Board of Trustees. Consult local legal counsel for state variations in the role and status of Boards of Trustees.

Most missions do not need separate accounts, especially if the total budget is less than $500,000. Because of the complexity and importance of the work of the Board of Trustees, strong leaders with a mission mind-set will provide a healthy balance between the costs of property

7 John Topolewski, "Mr. Wesley's Trust Clause: Methodism in the Vernacular," *Methodist History* 37, no. 3 (April 1999): 146–47, citing Jonathon Crowther, *A Portraiture of Methodist, or The History of the Wesleyan Methodists* (London: Richard Edwards, 1815), 307. For updated language, see also "Church Property Section 1: All Titles-In Trust," in *The Discipline*, ¶2501.

management and missional priorities. For trustees, stewardship is an ever-present reality.

Reflection Questions

1. If you have ever served on one of these leadership teams, share the most positive experience you had in that role.
2. What kind of person would you want to serve in a leadership position in your church?
3. What does faithful stewardship look like in your setting? How do you appreciate and affirm your leaders? How could leaders be thanked for their service?
4. If Jesus was one of your volunteers or on a leadership team, how would he describe the experience?
5. Should church leaders have term limits? What are the advantages and disadvantages?
6. What is your mission's greatest leadership need? Name five things to do to meet that leadership need.

CHAPTER EIGHT

COMMUNICATION

I get a liberating, elevating, duplicating, formulating lift;
I gave back what I got from God and there's a lot to spare.[1]

Does your communication about finances express hope or assume the worst? Are you avoiding communicating things that diminish, impair, and restrict giving? Honest reflection about communication will reveal new strategies for sharing hope and confidence that inspires generosity so that our missions thrive.

Stewardship defines the lifestyle of disciples who welcome others to share a vision to change the world. Our stewardship must also include practices and activities that cultivate generosity for funding missions and demonstrating the impact of gifts of time, prayers, and money. Consider what the following statements communicate about money and its role in our lives and faith communities:

- Stewardship is our spiritual discipline as recipients of God's generosity.
- Money is a tool for accomplishing God's vision.
- A person's need to give and share is more important than the need of the mission to receive.

---

1 From "God Multiplies Your Gifts," *Sardines and Biscuits,* copyright 2009. For full lyrics and to order music, email Mitch.Thomas@LACLT.com.

- Giving is our response to God in recognition of gifts we have already received.

Kennon L. Callahan offers two guiding principles for financial stewardship. He says, "Congregations never have enough money," and "Congregations have all the money they really need for God's mission."[2] Churches have regular contact with their donors, sometimes as often as weekly, creating communication opportunities envied by other organizations. Additional opportunities to communicate include newsletters, financial statements, pastoral visits, and small group settings such as Bible studies and various affinity groups. Are these opportunities nurtured or neglected?

We are blessed with many options for communicating our stories about mission. Even with life's questions and worries, our faith declares the continuing presence of God in our midst. Our stewardship and financial communications are faith statements that need to focus on hope and gratitude in all times.

Back Porch/Front Porch

This simple metaphor offers wisdom about our communication, especially about money. People typically present themselves to their neighborhood via their front porch. Often decorated with plants, outdoor furniture, or seasonal decorations, our front porch reflects the image of ourselves we wish the community to see. Our back porch is less orderly, more informal. It might be a storage location for broken furniture, extra plant pots, or even trash on its way to the garage. Shielded with more privacy, the back porch—garage or shed—is where our unfinished work and refuse often land as they transition to another place or out of our lives, and where we expect a higher level of privacy and confidentiality.

Now, visualize the front porch and the back porch of your mission or faith community. How are we presenting ourselves to the community? Is the image you see a good representation of what we would like to communicate? Or are back-porch activities taking place in the more public front porch?

2 Kennon Callahan, *Finance and Stewardship in an Effective Church* (Nashville, TN: Abingdon Press, 1992), 4.

Confusion about the boundaries of topics appropriate to the back porch and front porch challenges how others see us and our mission. Difficult conversations and decisions with financial or personnel implications require a degree of back-porch confidentiality. Public airing of grievances or parking-lot conversations about important matters are often back-porch conversations being held in front-porch settings. Balancing fellowship norms and professional boundaries requires clear understanding about communications on both the back porch and front porch.

Congregations where boundaries are unknown, unclear, or unprotected find themselves cleaning up messes rather than strengthening their mission. Privileged communication requires us to set boundaries and uphold covenants of confidentiality to protect our reputation and morale. I like to remind leaders that when they say "The ship is sinking," we shouldn't be surprised when the rats flee. Appropriate and helpful communication can strengthen or undermine our reputation and church morale, qualities directly linked to the generosity we try to inspire. The old adage is true: "If you can't say something nice, don't say anything at all."

Consistent and Compelling

Throughout the year and regardless of gift amounts, donors need information about the missions supported by their giving, including special campaigns and second-mile giving opportunities. Share information highlighting mission updates through giving statements, personalized letters, phone calls, newsletters, and website notices. Make sure that reporting and the plans of the finance and stewardship committees are transparent and that all communication is designed to clearly articulate challenges with consistent and compelling language. Consider making budget presentations narratives; as you present, illustrate with stories and testimonials about your mission. Make your communication positive, and frame challenges as opportunities that your church can face with faith.

Our mission work requires clear and inspiring communication in order to inform donors about the impact and results of their giving. Even a simple addition or improvement to communication can trigger generosity, inspiring hope. Consider the following communication opportunities: offertory invitations, bulletin inserts, newsletters, small-group studies and classes, workshops and presentations, person emails, letters, thank-you notes, visits from key church leaders and the pastor, testimonials given during worship, quarterly statements to donors. Don't forget displays in the gathering spaces and classrooms; pictures, charts, and other visuals on the walls; video clips as people come into worship or during the announcement time. It is especially effective to use video to show people well known to the church actively participating in mission.

In addition to helpful information, remember to frequently share inspirational stories and words of gratitude. Thank people for their service, but be careful; some people will not want to be thanked publicly, so check ahead of time. Positive messaging will transform morale, self-esteem, and generosity. Using **Worksheet 20. Communication and Celebration Goals**, plan steps for promoting your missional priorities.

Many skills and training resources strengthen interpersonal dialogue and effective communication, yet miscommunication still impacts ministry and relationships in significant ways. As most people realize, different life experiences, cultures, and languages influence communication, so remember to be sensitive and attentive; we may not realize when our communication is incomplete, unclear, or offensive to others. As our world becomes more diverse, multicultural, and multilingual, our communication skills must adapt. Because unresolved conflict is the leading cause of congregational decline, efforts to strengthen these skills are in our best interest. Consider these attributes that influence and complexify communication: language, leadership style, personality, gender, age, education, culture, personal history, birth order, neighborhood, profession, economic status, and faith.

Customizing Donor Communications

Best practices of stewardship recognize that donors are not all the same, so our communication must be customized to meet each donor and member where they are in their faith journey, even those who may not actively participate in our mission and ministry. In some churches, less active or lapsed members receive a variety of contacts, including letters sent with self-addressed stamped envelopes for convenient return. This shows that the church values their input and worship attendance more than financial support. I have even heard pastors say, "If you think all we want is your money, keep it."

The idea is to be systematic and intentional about communicating with specific donors and members. Communication with inactive people is done one way. Occasional attendees who have not made giving commitments can receive multiple communications that emphasize the joy of giving to God as an act of worship, as well as tips on the benefits of giving commitments with sensitivity to personal finance matters. Members who have joined during the past twelve months should receive personalized communications that recognize their discipleship journey toward joyful giving. Members who regularly attend worship and serve in a variety of ways deserve communication challenging them to grow toward tithing or a joyful giving goal. The goal is to cultivate and encourage lead donors who are generous with their time, testimony, tithes, and special offerings. Visits and personalized communications acknowledge the accomplishments, impact, and joy of their generosity as well as to challenge continuing growth in giving.

Another way to cultivate and organize communication is to group people by communication circles for specific types of contact and follow-up commitments; for example, people to visit, people to call, people to text, and people to reach via social media. Because people want to receive their information in different ways and because they respond to different forms of inspiration and challenge, consider the groups below and how to introduce stewardship practices and disciplines aligned with their particular life stages. Adapt each idea as needed to fit your culture.

Children and youth learn to appreciate generosity through experiential projects such as Heifer Arks and collecting coins. They can participate in a variety of giving rituals, including worship participation through ushering, liturgical processions, leading the offering dedication, testimonials, or fundraising for mission projects. Discovering they can participate, ask adults for support, and raise funds for mission are powerful leadership skills that last a lifetime.

Challenge adults to deepen their stewardship awareness by offering testimonials, serving as offering counters, learning about percentage giving, and tithing using a tithing chart or step chart summarizing current giving levels. Some faith communities hold dinners or meetings with different levels of donors or offer appropriate recognition and invitations. Expressing appreciation recognizes the diversity of gifts within congregations and inspires generosity. Some pastors and church leaders host coffees in their homes to talk about stewardship and promote mission.

Study group discussions or presentations on different aspects of stewardship invite people to deepen their understanding of giving as a spiritual discipline. Study materials and curricula on generosity, consumerism, personal finances, and mission opportunities are bountiful. Workshops, educational materials, or informal gatherings introduce planned giving and estate planning, gift annuities, wills, and donor-designated funds as tools for generous living. Community participation in educational projects cultivates new relationships and new mission partners.

New members need to be introduced to spiritual disciplines and giving opportunities immediately. Invite financial commitments during membership classes or orientation as part of discipleship. Give offering envelopes or commitment cards during orientation classes or membership exploration sessions while attention is strongest. But be sure that you don't focus only on financial stewardship. Christian stewardship also includes prayers, presence, gifts other than money, service, and witness. Hospitality extended through new member classes or dinners, orientation sessions, invitations to participate in worship, mission projects, or simply hearing giving and tithing stories cultivates commitment and generosity.

Narrative Budget: A Mission-Oriented Budget Presentation

Missions often fail to communicate the value of the services they provide and the impact on personal lives. Members and supporters often have a limited understanding of how their gifts translate into mission and almost no relationship with those benefiting from your missions. The line item budget effectively supports the work of the finance leadership and those managing resources. However, line items do not effectively interpret, communicate, or give witness to your mission and how lives are changed.

A narrative budget transforms your line item budget into a faith-in-action story using easy-to-understand descriptive ministry categories and visuals and offering an exciting and enlivening picture of your missional engagement. A narrative budget shows what you are doing in mission, discipleship training, benevolences, and ministry. It effectively connects the donor to your mission and serves as a marketing and orientation tool focusing on your missional activities. A well-composed narrative budget educates and inspires everyone. **Worksheet 24** provides instructions for creating a narrative budget presentation.

In addition to converting the line item budget to a creative visual, such as a pie chart, customized narratives tell your mission story in categories readers easily understand. The following two samples of category narratives offer examples of informative and inspiring mission stories.

- **Community/Fellowship.** This mission area encompasses how we care for one another and serve our community. During summer socials, movie nights, Rally Day, and Harvest Dances we enjoy fellowship with one another and welcome our neighbors. Sunday morning fellowship time offers healthy refreshments as well as relaxed time to visit with old and new friends. This year, our new Garden Club sprang to life yielding fresh, healthy vegetables for members and friends. Our harvest also supports food pantries for persons who find food security challenging. Other small groups include the Rocking Knitters, Book Club, Singles Dining Group, and Men's Group. Other groups form regularly, so bring your talents and share in our fellowship!
- **Pastoral Team.** Our gifted pastoral team coordinates the spiritual and temporal care of our faith community. Our lead pastor, Pastor Jane, shepherds us through exciting weddings, poignant funerals, and a variety of special ministry events including new summer studies, our annual Pie Auction, and our traditional Easter breakfast. Supporting families in crisis, hospital visits, and leading Bible study classes keep the pastoral team busy and magnifies the impact of our church. The ministry of our faith community includes empowerment of staff and volunteers. In our growing community, our pastors are both leaders and servants. Pastor Jane juggles these roles expertly as she and her team continue to learn and grow with us.

One alternative to a full narrative budget conversion is supplementing the budget with creative writing describing a mission area's leadership, activities, and goals as well as the financial commitment. This narrative presentation expands the line item budget into a story of who, what, and how mission occurs in your context. By expanding appreciation and information about how funds support mission, these narrative descriptions offer an interim step while moving toward a narrative budget resource. Here are two examples.

- **Christian Education Director, $8,000.** Forty percent of the Christian education budget provides supervision through the Christian Education Director for the seventy-five children attending Sunday school and receiving activity resources during worship. The children's safety and spiritual growth occurs in a cheerful environment with adult supervision as required by our Safe Sanctuaries Policy. Attendance awards, snacks, staff training, and curriculum planning are professional quality.
- **Education Supplies, $500.** Education Supplies funds the Sunday school curriculum, weekly prayer devotionals, adult Lenten study resources, Bibles for confirmands, and Vacation Bible School materials, such as art supplies.

Testimonials

Lead donors are good candidates for testimonies witnessing to the joy of giving. The following method for preparing someone to offer testimony is adapted from *The Stewardship Sourcebook.*[3] (Also see **Worksheet 23** for a testimonial planning tool.)

First, engage in prayer and read scripture to listen for wisdom and inspiration relating to your experience with God's generosity, presence, and assurance in your life. Focus on God's blessings and your encounters with stewardship and generosity. Reflect on any life-changing events you remember and persons who inspired or mentored you. Has your stewardship

3 Adapted from "Preparation of Lay Witness Presentations," in *Stewardship Sourcebook* (New Canaan, CT: Parish Publishing Inc. LLC, 2014), 41–42; www.parishpublishing.org. Used with permission.

commitment been challenged? How did you respond to those challenges? Identify the spiritual and personal changes in your life resulting from your stewardship response to God's generosity.

Second, draft your testimonial in an outline or narrative format. Consider introducing yourself, sharing your understanding of stewardship and God's generosity, sharing your personal story, and inviting others to experience the joy you have found through your generosity. Consider describing first-fruits giving rather than depending on what is left at the end of the month, sharing our innate need to give and to give thanks, drawing others in by valuing their experiences and capacity for joyful generosity, and emphasizing the joy and fulfillment of expressing our gratitude and trust in God by giving.

While testimonials are often used during stewardship campaigns, they are effective year-round. Keep these testimonies to three minutes. Because some people have difficulty keeping to a time limit, consider video recording and editing the testimony to the desired length. Then you can play the video at worship or use it in other settings with the person's permission. In my experience, a well-edited video actually enhances the person's witness.

Weekly Giving Reports

Some churches share weekly giving summaries that report income in comparison to the budget's needs. While in some settings this information is consistently positive, more often it communicates a discouraging message. Sharing some financial information is helpful when clear communication has not existed in the past or understanding about the financial reality is lacking. However, because the worship bulletin is a form of public communication, visitors and friends need to be inspired and affirmed in this setting. Financial challenges first need to be considered by the finance leaders. Then a positive plan, inviting partnership and leadership, is shared publicly. If financial information is shared weekly, find a way to give a positive message. Was giving stronger than the previous week, or the monthly average? Was giving stronger this year than last year for this week or month? Look creatively to find something positive to communicate. Then share that message.

Year-Round Stewardship

We typically undercommunicate regarding giving and finances. Whether constrained by worry, fear, or tradition, restricting financial stewardship communication to the annual pledge commitment process limits giving. God's generosity is always year-round. As stewards, we thank God every day and celebrate giving joyfully and throughout the year. Year-round stewardship reframes the typically annual financial commitment process to daily opportunities to honor God, making each day of our lives the right time to practice the spiritual disciplines of faithful stewardship. A wide range of definitions and practical examples of stewardship include increasingly creative options for moving beyond a fall giving appeal to an everyday, all-year-long culture of stewardship that promotes generosity. Create year-round stewardship strategies that align with your culture, history, and spiritual practices. Like discipleship, the stewardship journey continues each day of our lives and should be woven into all aspects of our mission.

The leadership skills and characteristics described below identify ways to share, proclaim, and affirm year-round stewardship disciplines. Consider each of these characteristics and assess the strength of these qualities in your setting. Improvements or growth in any of these year-round stewardship qualities or practices strengthens your mission!

Ask For It (AFI) and Challenge Goals: Year-round stewardship leaders honor the spiritual discipline of inviting everyone to set a personal giving commitment at least annually, using the tithe as a goal. Giving challenges may invite growing a percentage step toward tithing the resources God has provided. People are more likely to grow into generous lives when asked or invited. The most common reason for not giving is that no one asked! However, do not define year-round stewardship as a year without commitments, and again, emphasize that stewardship is more than thinking about money. Rather, stewardship focuses on God and how God wants us to spend not only money but also our time and talents. An estimated commitment is a healthy spiritual discipline and supports healthy budget building. Successful pastors also learn how appropriate invitations for extraordinary gifts or special projects throughout the year supplement giving commitments.

Attitude of Affirmation: Effective stewardship leaders inspire others, set realistic goals, have a positive attitude, and express their faithful hopes openly. Joyful affirmations and stories about gifts, blessings, and giving occur year-round. A positive, hopeful attitude infuses spoken affirmations, quotes and stories, articles, bulletin inserts, spoken and written testimonials, preaching, offertory invitations and rituals, humorous skits, and other creative liturgical acts. Mission moments given by laity or pastors regularly introduce ongoing mission projects and invite others to generously support efforts year-round. Communication about giving is consistently linked to mission activities.

Leaders Who Lead: Effective leaders understand they are role models, taking others to places they have never been before to do things they may not believe they can do. Year-round stewardship leaders become comfortable sharing their giving and tithing spiritual journey as well as aspects of their personal financial stewardship. Pastors place their giving envelope in the offering plate like the members. Knowing that the pastor contributes each week sends a powerful message to the congregation. This way we develop and value good listening habits as well as financial and budget management skills.

Worship Unabashedly Cultivates Generosity: Worship participants experience year-round stewardship through preaching, liturgy, and music celebrating God's generosity. Worship affirms our role and responsibility as stewards and reminds us that the stuff we accumulate often impedes our spiritual growth, maturity, and joy. Throughout the year, the liturgical seasons offer a framework for offering fresh perspectives on year-round stewardship. Advent and Lent are significant seasons for celebrating gifts and inviting sacrificial disciplines to benefit others. **Worksheet 21: A Liturgical Year Stewardship Framework** offers one way to align stewardship principles to the liturgical calendar year. Challenge yourself to find a stewardship dimension to every scripture passage–the possibilities are abundant. **Worksheet 22. Year-Round Stewardship Planning Calendar** offers a framework for planning your yearly activities and themes. Your definition and experience with year-round stewardship is as diverse as your missional visions and priorities; it is an attitude more than an activity. Explore boldly!

Reflection Questions

1. Describe the types of communication you find most inspiring. Are you experiencing or receiving that type of communication in your church?
2. How do you prefer to receive your information about meetings, updates, and other communications?
3. Consider creating a Bible study to look at what Jesus says about money.
4. We communicate all the time. Consider the ways you communicate or do not communicate about the missions you support. Identify three ways you will practice communicating a missional message this week. Who is your target audience, and what will you communicate?
5. List the passages from the Bible or your spiritual practices that give you hope. Compare that list to the message you hear at church. What are the similarities? What are the differences?
6. As a steward of God's creation and God's message of love, name something you feel called to support in a new way. Who will you tell?
7. What is a mission that gets you excited? Why?

CHAPTER NINE

PRACTICES FOR PROTECTING ALL PARTIES

Policies and Procedures

"For I know the plans I have for you," declares the LORD, *"plans to prosper you and not to harm you, plans to give you hope and a future."*

—Jeremiah 29:11

Don't ever think the mother
who lets you hold her baby
isn't watching how you hold it.

—Steve Garnaas-Holmes

I used to think that institutional memory would last at least three years. I now realize it may not last three months. Have you noticed how frequently we recount changes implemented two or three years ago, believing they occurred last year? Organizational documentation stating expectations, priorities, and covenants is the best antidote to forgetfulness, providing a safety net and clarification when questions arise. In this chapter, we will briefly review legal responsibilities and a documentation storage system called a *permanent file*. Then we will offer summary descriptions of organizational policies, including information about the purpose of each recommended policy. The appendices that follow this final chapter offer additional information and examples of these policies that can help you develop your priorities and covenantal expectations.

Ongoing administrative tasks, such as updating policies, preparing for financial audits, and ensuring compliance with local, state, and federal laws is daunting. However, these disciplines affect our mission capacity, health, and ability to reach our mission's fullest potential. Once established, the policies described here require ongoing monitoring and periodic updates. Paying attention to these administrative tasks will strengthen your mission by reducing conflict and providing protection for staff and volunteers. The importance of policies and documentation for healthy financial stewardship will increase for the following reasons.

- Government and regulatory agencies show increasing interest in nonprofits, including church compliance with changing laws, regulations, and our adopted policies.
- Audits and financial-procedure reviews teach best practices and restore trust, integrity, and donor confidence contributing to mission growth. Those without annual audits face increasing risk and vulnerability and are ineligible for some funding sources.
- Policies must be reviewed annually to keep language and principles current. Noncompliance with adopted policies puts all of us at risk.

Legal Responsibilities

As nonprofit organizations, our missions have a variety of privileges and responsibilities, including expectations by the United States government. Your EIN (Employer Identification Number) and tax-exempt status fall under the federal government's jurisdiction. Please note that there are variations in state and local legal and taxation regulations regarding registering as a nonprofit in the state where business is conducted, state authorization to raise funds for your mission, employee compensation requirements including minimum wages, and worker's compensation insurance and other insurances. The Internal Revenue Service, your Secretary of State's office, and your city or town clerk's offices all support your navigation through these legal responsibilities. Becoming familiar with the federal, state, and local regulations that apply to nonprofits is one aspect of accountable stewardship.

Audit and Annual Review

Nonprofit organizations conduct annual audits and financial-procedure reviews. Audits require full disclosure of financial assets and resources, which ensures integrity and professional stewardship practices and increases donor confidence and generosity. Because audits can generate anxiety, the following observations may be helpful. Consider viewing the annual audit and review, an annual accountability discipline, like a visit to the dentist. The anticipatory anxiety a dental visit generates usually far exceeds the actual experience. Despite our temptation to avoid it, the resulting clean teeth and fresh breath really are satisfying. When there is pain or disease, the sooner it is dealt with the better. Often recommendations are minor adjustments, but serious work is sometimes needed. A life of attentiveness to the dentist's recommendations prevents some serious problems. *Now rephrase the last five sentences, replacing "a dental visit" with an "annual audit."*

The anticipatory anxiety an audit generates usually far exceeds the actual experience. Despite our temptation to avoid it, the resulting clean audit and verified procedures really are satisfying. When there are problems or findings, the sooner it is dealt with the better. Often recommendations are minor adjustments, but serious work is sometimes needed. A life of attentiveness to the auditor's recommendations prevents some serious problems. *Uncanny, isn't it?*

Each year, millions of dollars, faithfully given to missions, are misappropriated. While some people succumb to temptation, most organizations do not adequately safeguard their finance staff and volunteers. When misconduct happens, organizations also bear responsibility if they don't follow best practices for safeguarding resources and people. If you are still worried about asking about your last audit, take a moment to think about the times we place our lives in the hands of others to conduct tests and complete life-saving procedures. An audit or review may feel like placing your mission under a microscope, but the truth is that what we don't know could destroy everything. Committing to good financial stewardship practices includes allowing others to review our recordkeeping to ensure everyone's safety. While this will require trust, your peace of mind and your staff's safety is worth it.

While the scope and scale of your financial review and audit depends on your mission size and complexity, all audits review three different but related financial management processes: (1) tracking movement of funds or money; (2) reviewing reports for content and clarity; and (3) reviewing policies and procedures for financial stewardship, including property and asset management. (See **Appendix A** for more detailed information about the audit and review process.)

Taxes

Churches and ministries of The United Methodist Church are granted nonprofit status by the IRS under a Private Letter Ruling. This status grants a variety of privileges as well as obligations. Additional information is available online and through denominational resources, such as the General Council on Finance and Administration (GCFA). While churches enjoy tax-exempt status, they are still accountable for a variety of taxes based on mission activities. Having employees triggers payroll taxes; certain sales activities trigger sales taxes; and in some areas, local jurisdictions impose property taxes. Check carefully to ensure your records and financial procedures include caring for appropriate tax filings and insurance coverages, including income tax, employee identification, and withholding forms, as well as quarterly payment of withheld income taxes, worker's compensation, health insurance, and property insurance. Other fees or taxes may apply, so always check local ordinances or regulations.

Being a nonprofit does not release us from federal and state employee laws. Any persons hired must complete tax withholdings and identity verification forms. Reports are required that verify income, withholdings, and other tax-related information, including housing exclusions. Clergy housing exclusions require prior approval by the governing body—Charge Conference—and face ongoing legal challenges. The housing exclusion benefit, the impact of a parsonage, and reimbursable business expenses documentation complexify clergy taxes. Clergy, especially United Methodist clergy, should seek a tax professional with experience filing United Methodist clergy tax returns.

Employee vs. Contractor

Employees and contractors have different work expectations and paperwork. Criteria for determining whether employee or contractor status is appropriate should be carefully evaluated and understood. Resources are available online and should always be checked to verify status determination. Contractors complete different tax forms and receive different tax reporting documents (specifically, a 1099) than do employees. Most United Methodist clergy are employees and receive a W-2 form, which includes housing exclusion and additional housing support if not in a parsonage. Because United Methodist clergy are also considered self-employed for Social Security purposes, additional taxes apply. Again, clergy taxes and United Methodist benefits are complex; always consult a tax preparer who is familiar with the denominational clergy compensation.

Church Reporting

In addition to reports related to employee or contractor compensation, churches with employees must submit quarterly income-tax withholdings to the IRS using Form 945. Currently, churches do not need to submit Form 990 because of the IRS private-letter ruling status. However, legal challenges to this status may lead to changes that will impact church taxes and filing status. Some ministries have begun filing 990s voluntarily, which requires disclosure of income sources, including donors. Annually, donor giving statements are sent to each donor by January 31, verifying total contributions and whether they are tax deductible. As this information is subject to change, always check local and federal requirements

Permanent File

Protect important documents and ensure access to organizational records for future generations by creating a permanent file. Place the mission's important documentation in a secure fireproof cabinet accessible for future leaders, auditors, and the governing body. The contents, described below, should be reviewed regularly and updated with current information.

A. Church Property Deeds and Surveys

1) Should always include United Methodist Church Trust Clause language.

2) Check state laws regarding church name records. If the name is changed by the denomination, the change is valid (i.e., Methodist Episcopal Church is the same as The United Methodist Church). State laws may require creating a new deed with all previous deeds deeding to The United Methodist Church.

3) Surveys of property and buildings conducted to identify architecture, utilities, environmental or historic data, and title searches, noting any changes that have occurred.

4) Check deeds for reversion clauses, which prevent property sale, because when the property is no longer used by the church, it reverts back to the grantors.

B. Cemetery Information

1) Deeds.

2) Policies describing who can be buried, what can be erected or put on site temporarily or permanently, and maintenance expectations and rules.

3) Columbarium construction and policies for disposition of cremains.

C. Incorporation documents, if required. Check state incorporation policies because nonprofits and churches may have different statutes. For example, Maine has a statute incorporating all Methodist churches under one statute. Some states, like New Jersey, require an entity to be incorporated to hold title to property.

D. By-laws: Missions agencies will have articles of incorporation and by-laws. United Methodist churches use the current version of the *Book of Discipline* as their by-laws.

E. The General Council on Finance and Administration 501 (c) (3) Private Letter Ruling that identifies United Methodist churches as nonprofit entities since 1974. Some missions need to request a restatement for their inclusion in the umbrella status. New church starts need to request inclusion of their EIN to the Private Letter Ruling umbrella.

F. Federal Employer Identification Number (EIN) required for all filings, including employee taxes and tax-exempt status.

G. Leases or use agreements with all groups or individuals who are not programs of the church such as Scouting groups, AA, nursery schools, school programs, private music recitals, and so on. A lease agreement is necessary, even if there is no rent.

1) Lease includes information about payments, access/keys, responsibilities, cancellation policy, insurance, and so on. The lease will also include building-use rules and expectations.

2) Rental agreement or building-use agreements for any group using the building for a couple of hours.

3) Churches should never lease to an entity that is not a tax-exempt 501 (c) (3), per US federal law. Any church engaging in any activity with any entity that is not a tax-exempt 501 (c) (3) may risk their own property tax-exemption status and engage in taxable activity (Unrelated Business Income Tax).

4) Parsonage's location and information (*Book of Discipline* ¶2503). Parsonage rental agreements should be reviewed by legal counsel and may trigger tax implications if not used for a missional purpose. Parsonages' sales have additional disciplinary requirements of approval by conference judicatories and district superintendents.

5) Retain copies of the 501 (c) (3) documentation and insurance binder (verification of insurance coverage) from any groups or tenants using church-owned buildings or property.

H. Insurance policies: Retain documentation that verifies each year's payment of and coverage for

1) property insurance, including replacement, liability, and other appropriate coverage;

2) health insurance, including verification of any coverage provided to staff or pastor; and

3) vehicle insurance, if applicable.

I. Property tax exemption: Some states require periodic reapplication for property tax exemption.

J. Titles for all vehicles and dates when registration, inspection, and insurance expire.

K. State Sales Tax Exemption Form.

L. Copies of all letters sent to donors for their tax deductions for previous two years.

M. Bank accounts: Numbers, statements, and the names listed as signers with each financial institution.

N. Investments: Account numbers and summary of all assets, including Endowment Funds and Trusts and signers or authorized contact persons.

O. Copies of all donor-restricted bequests to the church through wills and trusts.

P. Employee information and filings.

Q. Church policies, including but not limited to Safe Sanctuary, fire drills, and so on.

R. Current Charge/Church Conference report booklet with budget, audit, and nominations information.[1]

Policies

Because trust is fragile and finances cause more worry than security, disclosures about questionable actions and decisions undermine the generosity we need for our missional success. These financial policy descriptions outline each policy's purpose, including protection and documentation helpful to those who will steward God's resources after we are gone. As legal requirements and regulations change and vary by state or region, always consult local professionals for any necessary modifications or adaptations. This story highlights the importance of policies and procedures that protect people and encourage generosity.

1 This list created by Evelynn S. Caterson, Esq., Chancellor, Greater New Jersey Annual Conference, 2018. Used with permission.

True Story: I finally managed to call a Finance Committee meeting. I couldn't put my finger on the reason for the uneasiness in the room. I noticed there was no report on the invested funds. They were reluctant to even tell me the amount invested. The real story surfaced after we finished our business and a married couple lingered.

He asked, "Can they [the Conference] take our money away from us?" I assured him *they* could not. He then promised to bring his binders with investment statements to our first Trustees meeting next week, so at least he trusts me enough to show me the account information that I had told him I needed to see.

When a new United Methodist church was built nearby, parishioners were afraid their money would be *taken*. I think this is the reason they keep their investments local and refuse other Conference-related investment options. Who has perpetrated this belief? How easy it could have been to relieve their fears and give them a better return on their investments over the past eight years. I've been told nobody in the church knows how much the church has invested—that the amount of interest is all the church folk need to know. This is all because they are afraid the Conference will take their money if they reveal how much money they have.

People's feelings are rather fragile. They do seem to trust me, though, which is a good beginning. For instance, the fellow who cared for memorial gifts died in June. The woman who took over had no idea what to do and started putting the money in general funds. I was able to help her to understand the process that needs to be followed with memorials, so I think that will be properly cared for now.[2]

2 Shared with permission by Pastor Elizabeth Bailey-Mitchell, People's United Methodist Church in Union and Searsmont United Methodist Church, ME.

Local United Methodist church policies are adopted by the governing body, also known as the Charge Conference. Documents presented for adoption are written as *resolutions* or *proposals*, which are then considered, revised if needed, and adopted as official policy. Some policies are then signed by leaders or the presiding elder or district superintendent. Once approved and signed as official policies guiding decision making in the future, copies should be filed in multiple locations, including a permanent file.

Adopting policies for financial procedures or gift or fund management gives leaders guidance about how to respond in different situations. Creating plans and policies greatly reduces confusion and conflict while at the same time encouraging generosity to support your missions.

Building-Use Policy

When another group uses church property, a *building-use policy* clarifies expectations about access to the property and use of facilities, such as food preparation, sound systems, worship space activities and supplies, set-up and clean-up expectations, safety, and insurance verification. Information on fees, keys, and emergency contacts are important policy elements. Any users need to align with your missional purpose and provide a *binder* documenting appropriate insurance coverage. Uses that are not missional could trigger taxes for unrelated business income. Property use may generate significant income, and careful attention to nonprofit regulations and legal considerations will reduce potential risks.

Endowment Policy

Language contained in your endowment policy should include a description of membership, the purpose of the endowment, an investment policy, and guidelines for amending the policy. Also known as a *charter*, the policy defines the goals, framework, and identified priorities for an endowment in your mission. Because of the legal responsibilities and financial accountability for managing invested assets and endowments, the policy contains language similar to by-laws. Legal counsel is recommended to ensure this policy complies with state laws impacting investments, endowments, and charitable giving by nonprofit organizations.

Finance Policy

Providing instructions for creating the budget, opening bank accounts, managing transactions, recordkeeping, and other aspects of financial management, your finance policies orient leaders to mission procedures and expectations. While roles and responsibilities for financial management are defined in the *Book of Discipline*, these policies provide supplemental guidance for local operations.

Gift-Acceptance Policy

This policy offers donors and committees guidance about the types of gifts accepted and how different types of gifts are stewarded, including refusing certain gifts. Especially appreciated by major donors, the policy provides helpful guidance describing whether valuable items or property could be donated to your mission. This policy helps your mission avoid gifts it can't use.

Memorial Fund Policy

Memorial funds receive gifts honoring a person's life. The memorial fund policy describes the purpose and stewardship of gifts, appropriate uses, and local traditions. Input from family members may be invited; however, the church retains the right to adopt or reject suggestions. Since families and members cannot create new designated funds, requesting input does not supersede the church's authority to make the final decision. Affirm the life and values of the lives honored by having a plan and avoiding accumulating memorial funds without a clear plan or process.

Pastor's Discretionary Fund Policy

This designated fund is often available to pastors for special needs or pastoral care emergencies. Models for funding, managing, and distributing discretionary funds vary. Pastors should never be sole signatures on a discretionary-fund account. This practice puts both the church and the pastor in a position of unnecessary risk and temptation. It is the church's responsibility to protect both its assets and leadership. Periodically review the fund-management system to ensure all parties understand the procedures and the pastor is protected from tax or misappropriation risk.

> ***True Story***: When the new pastor increased the clarity regarding how and where special offerings for

discretionary pastoral care were received and deposited, one donor immediately gave a check for $1,000. The new system included simple boxes from the craft store that clearly identified these designated gifts and assured donors of the careful stewardship of their generosity, which generated even more generosity.[3]

Are your donors getting clear signals about the stewardship of their gifts?

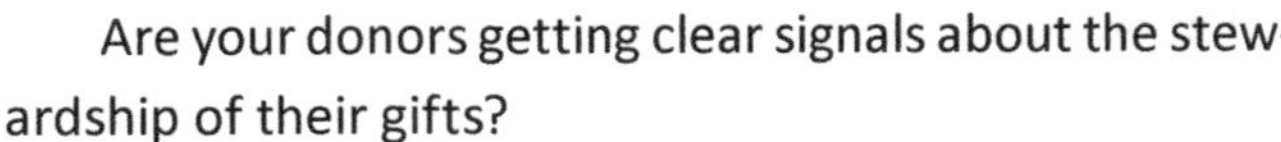

Whether called a discretionary fund, emergency fund, friendly aid fund, or assistance fund, if pastoral staff give financial assistance to any person in need, the characteristics and the responsibilities described below apply. Additional information is provided to encourage best practices.

Funding a Discretionary Fund: The financial secretary records incoming money to a discretionary fund as income. This recordkeeping ensures that gifts are income to the mission, not inadvertently taxable income to the pastor or executive director. Discretionary funds may be included in the annual budget or funded by a special offering, such as Communion Sundays, or by gifts in recognition of birthdays or other special events. Designating as income other special offerings or gifts to the church received for weddings, baptisms, or funeral services are other options. However, these gifts in recognition of a service provided must be given to the church. If the payment is made in the pastor's name, it becomes taxable income for the pastor. Your fund policy describes how a pastor's discretionary fund is funded.

Dispersals from the Discretionary Fund: Funds to aid individuals or families are given in ways that protect the confidentiality of the recipients while also protecting the pastor from unnecessary risk. Some pastors give aid and submit a voucher to the treasurer for reimbursement, while others submit a voucher in advance. Some pastors keep a record of all transactions and submit a summary report, which the treasurer holds confidentially. Because clergy have discretion regarding the distribution of funds, a confidential record indicating when and to whom funds were dispersed is in their best

3 Shared with permission by Pastor Elizabeth Bailey-Mitchell.

interest. Payments should never be made in the name of the pastor. Pastors should expect to be asked to account for funds distributed, even funds authorized for confidential distribution of aid.

Providing in-kind assistance (for example, purchasing a bag of groceries or a train ticket rather than giving cash) is recommended. Pastors and leaders should discuss vouchers or gift cards for food or transportation options appropriate to their local context.

Leaders may request some type of report on discretionary fund distribution. Summary reports describe the needs met and maintain confidentiality about the recipient's identity. For example, a report of $300 in food assistance to six families and two nights' housing assistance for a family of four gives valuable feedback about needs while maintaining confidentiality. The policy indicates when and what is reported for future planning purposes and clarity about community needs. Since financial support is a valuable way missions support individuals and families in our communities, healthy management of the discretionary fund is essential. Doing God's work in this world requires accountability and responsibility.

WHAT ARE THE RISKS OF THE FOLLOWING POLICY LANGUAGE AND WHY IS THIS NOT RECOMMENDED?

The pastor shall maintain a separate checking account to manage the discretionary funds. The treasurer shall remit designated discretionary funds to this checking account as requested by the pastor. The balance in this checking account shall be reviewed by the Finance Committee at least once a year. This checking account shall not be used for the pastor's personal or business expenses. The discretionary fund checking account shall be audited annually.

Answer: Even with careful accounting, the IRS could force the pastor to report this as personal taxable income.

Safe Sanctuary and Limited Access Policies

Faith communities set expectations about protecting children, youth, and other vulnerable persons by adopting a Safe Sanctuary policy with guidelines for supervision, adult-child ratios, and transportation. After adoption, annual review and revisions, as well as ongoing education, are necessary. In situations where previous violations of trust, convictions of illegal actions, or status as an offender of some sort exist, customized agreements or covenants set expectations for any level of access or activity. Such covenants need ongoing supervision and vigilance, and set appropriate boundaries seeking safety for all persons. This policy is included because it is a best practice to reduce the financial and legal consequences of violations of trust or of misconduct.

These policies protect all parties and provide important guidance when leadership has questions or finds itself in situations requiring difficult decisions or choices. However, their usefulness is limited to their use by leaders. Annual review of all policies is an important discipline to practice and necessary to ensure that awareness and actions align with adopted plans and expectations. Having a policy provides no protection if the policy is not followed, and as culture shifts and we learn more about accountability and safety, annual reviews keep this documentation up to date. Leaders interested in protecting their people and missions make sure policies exist and are kept current. In addition, building your mission's integrity, avoiding conflict, and demonstrating professional financial stewardship strengthen donor confidence and build generosity.

Reflection Questions

1. How do you conduct the annual audit? What is your procedure? Does it need to be reviewed?
2. Are your policies up to date? If not, create a schedule for review, revision, and the needed approvals.
3. Who is protected by your policies and procedures?
4. This chapter recommends a permanent file. Who do you need to work with to create that backup system?
5. How does this chapter on policies connect to your stewardship ministry and your efforts to cultivate generosity?
6. When Jesus calls and asks how your ministry protected its leaders, how will you respond?

BENEDICTION

To those terrified of talking about money,
  a blessing for courage.
To those curious about money,
  a blessing for creative exploration of possibilities.
To those oblivious to the control money has over their lives,
  wisdom for personal stewardship.
To those planning well who worry about planning well enough,
  confidence in God's provision.
To those experiencing a call to teaching financial stewardship,
  opportunities to learn and be heard.
To all stewards,
  a blessing for knowledge, wisdom, grace, and courage
  aligning your financial stewardship with spiritual disciplines
  transforming our fears into faith every day.

—Bonnie Ives Marden

APPENDICES

Description and Disclaimer

The following appendices contain additional information about topics briefly introduced earlier, including additional descriptions and sample language for developing policies and documentation for future leaders. This material is only for educational purposes.

When using any of this information for the creation of policies, consultation with local professionals and legal counsel is strongly encouraged to ensure alignment with local statutes and applicable regulations. Policies and legal principles change and often vary in different locations. Consultation ensures policy language is appropriate for your location.

Any use of these samples without legal counsel places all responsibility on the user for any unforeseen consequences. Users may find significant changes are required by local or state regulations. Once adopted, annual review of policies ensures both accuracy and awareness of procedures and expectations.

Appendix J. Worksheets provides all of the worksheets referenced in the text.

APPENDIX A
AUDIT INFORMATION

Your annual audit review ensures accuracy in financial bookkeeping and assures donors of the responsible stewardship of their generosity.[1] This accountability activity includes two main tasks: (1) determining the current *value of all accounts*, including money and property, and (2) testing *financial procedures, policies, and documentation*. The process documents all accounts, assets, investments, CDs, stocks, and property owned, managed, or stewarded. Churches may be exempt from some financial reports required of other nonprofit organizations, but statutes vary by state, and audits are required by law and by denominational polity. All gifts, bequests, memorial funds, or trustee funds, unless stated otherwise in a will or legal document, are included in the annual audit's balance sheet. When income is generated from assets managed by another entity on behalf of the church, the fund value can be reported, noting the current fund manager or trustee. The exception is that in current United Methodist polity, United Methodist Women's funds are reported in the audit, but they may choose to audit separately.

The audit report includes a summary of all accounts and their balances recorded on a *fund balance* report. All accounts and their beginning and ending values with summaries of transactions are recorded. Account or fund balances come from bank or financial institution statements and should match the organization's accounting system records. The *fund balance report* of

---

1 Additional audit guidance is available for United Methodist churches at www.gcfa.org. The current Audit Guide is available at http://www.gcfa.org/forms-and-resources/financial-forms/.

account values documents the financial institution's account balances, not the church financial system's budget categories.

Then, the audit process compares the bank or financial institution fund records with the church accounting system records and assesses financial practices related to the financial management of money. Tests during this financial review seek to

- verify gifts made by donors match gift amounts recorded by the financial secretary;
- verify weekly deposit totals match bank deposit amounts;
- verify income amounts in church finance accounting match bank deposits;
- verify invoices for expenses match actual payments to vendors;
- verify expenses recorded in the church finance system match invoice amounts;
- verify donors' giving records match church records on gifts received;
- verify any other aspects of the financial systems reviewed; and
- note any discrepancies and adjust church balances and recordkeeping as needed.

The procedural review looks at *internal controls*, a variety of financial operational procedures. These expectations apply to churches of all sizes.

- Is weekly counting done by two unrelated adults from different households?
- Are deposits timely? Are offerings deposited on Sunday or Monday?
- Are pledges recorded on donor's records? Are quarterly statements sent?
- Is the status of pledges reviewed and reported to the pastor?
- Who has authority to sign checks, make online payments, and use credit cards?
- Do payments get authorized, dated, and coded for the accounts to be charged?
- Are invoices paid in a timely manner? Are any payments made more than thirty days after receipt? Are finance charges being incurred?

- Are expenditures within budget approved amounts? What happens when bills exceed approved budget amounts?
- Are local and federal payroll, tax, benefits, and recordkeeping regulations followed? Does each person have a separate file, and are I-9, CORI, W-2 or 1099 forms used appropriately? Are other legal forms stored securely?
- Are donor-restricted gifts tracked and accounted for appropriately? Are major gifts and bequests appropriately received and managed?
- Verify property and asset locations as well as debts.
- Verify where legal documents are stored and whether insurance coverage is sufficient.
- Are all assets reported annually in the Charge Conference report?
- Is the previous year's audit in Charge Conference report?
- Review all organization policies.

A narrative summary of the procedures tested and any findings leading to adjustments is created by the auditor or review team. Recommendations for improving financial procedures and systems are also noted with steps for implementation. Congregations should address any findings and implement appropriate adjustments to protect both assets and the people responsible for financial activities promptly. In the event of perceived errors or misconduct, further assessment occurs, followed by appropriate communication with institutional leadership so that legal counsel is obtained if needed. If the church has no budget, use bank statements to conduct the audit or review. When an audit has not been completed in several years, churches are encouraged to complete the most recent year first to reestablish annual audits. If issues are found during the process, previous years should also be reviewed. Leaders need to address any anxiety so that this important process is completed each year.

Information for Financial Audit and Procedures Review

Your auditor or audit review team will request the following documents for review. Maintaining good recordkeeping throughout the year helps keep these documents readily available.

- Copies of church policies and procedures related to finance and treasury functions and copies of minutes approving those policies.
- Copies of all the minutes from the Finance Committee, the Board of Trustees, the Administrative Board/Church Council, the previous Charge Conference(s), and the other entities (e.g., Local Church Foundation or endowment funds), and a list of persons holding the following positions: financial secretary and treasurer, as required; trustees treasurer, and memorial fund treasurer if applicable.
- List of all bank and investment accounts, including the person authorized to sign on each, and any designated accounts under the control of the pastor and in the name of the church.
- All financial reports for each month of the year, plus December of the previous year and January of the subsequent year—a fourteen-month period.
- All bank and investment account statements for the same period.
- Church reports and documentation of income and expenses. A printout of all transactions by account for the entire year, plus annual budget reports with approved and actual expenditures for the end of the previous year and the year being audited. If accounts are reconciled monthly, those reports are also reviewed.
- All paid invoices, payroll data, and files, including 941s, year-end W-2s, 1099s, and transmittal forms, income documentation, and deposit records for the fourteen-month period. Sample transactions are tested.
- The financial secretary's records and other income records for the same period. A monthly report of income with total deposited and broken down by categories is helpful. A sample of donor records is compared with weekly income reports and gift records in the church's recordkeeping system.

Some systems will be sampled and assessed further if needed. In summary, the audit compares the church's recordkeeping system to the financial institution or bank records and donors' records of gifts to the church.[2]

---

2 Adapted and excerpted from General Council of Finance and "Administration Local Church Audit Guide," available at http://www.gcfa.org/forms-and-resources/financial-forms/.

APPENDIX B
BUILDING-USE POLICY SAMPLE

This policy states the general guidelines for the use of [name of church] facilities and equipment. This policy was approved by [governing body] on [date].

General Guidelines

1. The facilities are for use by members and committees to accomplish our mission. Outside individuals and organizations whose activities are compatible with our mission may request use of the facilities. Our ministries will have priority over outside individuals or organizations.
2. All requests by outside individuals (non-members) or organizations will be referred to the Board of Trustees for consideration and authorization. The pastor must approve use of the facility for any religious activity. Organizations must coordinate their facility use with the Church Council.
3. Anyone using our facilities and grounds must conduct their activities and treat the facility as a house of worship. Smoking is prohibited. Consumption of alcoholic beverages or the possession of legally prohibited drugs is prohibited in the building or on the grounds. The property is maintained as a clutter-free environment by (1) storing material in storage areas and cabinets as designated by the Board of Trustees, and (2) coordinating displays and bulletin board communications with staff. Activity leaders are responsible for returning rooms used to their original arrangement.
4. All usage of the facility and grounds will comply with our Safe Sanctuary Policy for working with children and vulnerable populations.

Specific Areas

1. The sanctuary will generally be used only for worship activities. However, the pastor will have the authority to grant exceptions. Sufficient time for preparation for worship services shall be protected.
2. The fellowship hall and kitchen are for general use. Activities requiring these areas for extended periods require authorization. Use of the fellowship hall and kitchen will be coordinated with the church staff. Kitchen use will follow Kitchen Use Guidelines.
3. Separate use agreements will define any long-term arrangements for ongoing groups or missions such as child care/preschool or shared building users, and be reviewed at least annually in consultation with each group.

Use Approval Procedures for Church and Denominational Ministries

1. The Church Council coordinates ministry and work area activities requiring facility use.
2. The administrative assistant will maintain a schedule of facility reservations, including committees, members (e.g., weddings, funerals, family events, etc.), and other denominational groups, plus approved use by other individuals or organizations approved by the Board of Trustees. The administrative assistant, in consultation with the pastor and Church Council where necessary, will resolve schedule conflicts.
3. Church members or constituents and other groups sponsored by the district or annual conference offices may use the facilities without any financial contribution. For funerals, weddings, and other private events, a suggested contribution is encouraged to cover custodial and utility expenses.

Outside Organizations and Non-Members

1. Outside individuals or organizations requesting to use the facility submit a Church Facility Use Request Form seeking approval from the Trustees. The administrative assistant maintains all completed forms.

2. The Trustees, in consultation with the pastor, will evaluate all requests; private parties will not be approved.
3. Church staff and the Trustees assign available rooms, giving priority to our missions.
4. Outside organizations whose missions are determined to be supportive of a church mission area (e.g., evangelism or outreach) may use the facilities with no expected contribution as approved by the pastor and the Trustees.

To cover utility and custodial services, the church requests contributions from private individuals or organizations using the facilities if they are not associated with our mission. Customary contribution amounts are set by the Trustees.

Equipment

1. The Trustees have responsibility for managing all church equipment, such as tables and chairs, and equipment will be stored in designated areas and returned to storage areas after use.
2. The Kitchen Use Guidelines document controls the use of the kitchen and its equipment.
3. The church ministry areas and members have priority over outside organizations for equipment use.
4. Church members requesting to borrow equipment (e.g., tables, chairs) for personal use must have prior approval by staff. Each requestor will complete an Equipment Request Form approved and maintained by the administrative assistant.
5. Organizations requesting to borrow equipment must have the prior approval of the pastor or church staff. Requestor will complete an Equipment Request Form to obtain approval. The administrative assistant maintains records of equipment borrowed and returned. User will return equipment to the designated storage area and is financially responsible for repair or replacement if damaged.

Security

The security of our property is the responsibility of everyone using it. As a house of worship, no weapons or firearms are allowed.

Persons unlocking entrances take full responsibility to secure the entrance after use or delegate the responsibility to a trustworthy person. In the event a door cannot be secured, it must be immediately reported to the staff or a trustee.

Security Systems and Keys

1. Door key locks are the responsibility of the Trustees. A set of emergency keys is stored in an outside lock box for use by fire department and rescue personnel.
2. The Trustees are responsible for the access policy, including identifying groups and key duplication. The church staff will approve access to a church key. Persons requesting a key for the outside door locks must fill out a Key Access Form. The church administrative assistant will maintain records of approved access forms.
3. When a person leaves the church or no longer has access need, the key is returned to church staff, who record its return. The Trustees will conduct periodic inventories of authorizations and keys to ensure proper access control.
4. The property is protected by a fire alarm system. In the event of an alarm, all occupants are to exit the building in an orderly manner. The fire department is responsible for deactivating the system.

Supplemental Forms Related to Building Use

The following documents are noted above and should be created for your own ministry context:

- Kitchen Use Guidelines
- Church Facility Use Request Form
- Equipment Request Form
- Security Access/Key Form

APPENDIX C

ENDOWMENT POLICY INFORMATION AND SAMPLE

An endowment policy states the purpose and management plan for funds intended to be stewarded in perpetuity, that is, forever. The endowment policy expresses the desires and plans for the use of endowed funds, which may be invested. Samples of Endowment Policies for United Methodist churches are available through your local United Methodist Foundation and the National Association of United Methodist Foundation's endowment charter and policy template. For information about your area foundation, visit www.naumf.org/location/ or contact your annual conference office or local foundation.

Components of an Endowment Policy

An endowment policy describes the creation, purpose, management, responsibilities, and procedures for policy changes if needed in the future. The first section identifies the name of the fund, the state where it is located, and to whose laws or polity the fund is amenable. A description of the fund including undesignated or designated categories explains the purpose of the funds. Preferred sources of funding may be indicated as well as whether the fund is one large endowment or composed of several categories, for example, a music endowment and a mission endowment.

A management section describing how the endowment is to be administered provides language ensuring the endowment retains nonprofit status and clarifying who is responsible for its supervision and stewardship. References to applicable provisions in the Internal Revenue Code and applicable legislation and regulations ensure compliance with legal responsibilities.

The policy designates who is responsible for managing the fund. Options include the Board of Trustees, a subcommittee of the Trustees, an Endowment Committee, or a team of financial officers and other leaders. This group's membership, terms, nomination process, reporting and decision-making processes, and leadership structure are outlined in the policy.

Any instructions about the financial management or investment goals should be included (for example, whether investments are held to *socially responsible investing* principles). Limitations on use of the original gift—the principle—should be described for protection when financial challenges arise. Typical expectations are protection of principal, reasonable investment returns (income and dividends), and review of investments (e.g., companies, industries) by either the fund manager or the fund's supervising body.

Each endowment policy describes the method by which income from dividends or earned interest is used for current mission work. This *income or spending formula* may be based on market performance or on some other specified formula. Another important component of managing an endowment ministry is the *gifts acceptance policy,* which may be included in this policy. If a separate document, it offers guidance regarding other gifts that are not part of the endowment.

In United Methodist churches, the *Book of Discipline* authorizes the following powers and responsibilities:

1. To receive and administer all bequests received; to receive and administer all trusts; to invest all trust funds of the local church in conformity with laws of the country, state, or like political unit in which the ministry is located.
2. To emphasize the need for adults of all ages to have a will and an estate plan and to provide information on the preparation of these to all members.
3. To stress the opportunities for members and constituents to make provisions for giving through United Methodist Churches, institutions, agencies, and causes by means of wills, annuities, trusts, life insurance, memorials, and various types of property.
4. To arrange for the dissemination of information helpful in preretirement planning, including such considerations as establishing a living will and a

living trust, and the need to designate someone to serve as a responsible advocate should independent decision making be lost.

5. To update the committee rules and regulations after General Conference as needed.
6. Other responsibilities as determined by the Charge Conference.[1]

Finally, endowment policies describe the protections, such as bonding, and prohibition of payment for services in this work, gift acknowledgment, and earnings recordkeeping expectations, privacy and liability release, and how to amend the policy. Guidance about the disposition of the funds should the ministry, church, or judicatory merge or dissolve ensures future stewardship of funds. Additional legal language demonstrating amenability to local statutes, designating signers, and where the approved document is to be submitted and stored completes the policy document. Additional information is provided below for those just beginning to organize this ministry.

ORGANIZING AN ENDOWMENT MINISTRY: ROLES AND RESPONSIBILITIES

Organizing an endowment plan includes deciding how the fund is administered and invested and communicating this opportunity to donors for planned gifts supporting missional goals. The team leading this project will

1. recommend the types of activities the endowment supports (missions, education, building, etc.), usually based on future goals or long-term vision;
2. recommend what types of gifts will be accepted and manage the exploration and receipt of planned gifts on behalf of the mission, often in consultation with the Trustees;
3. recommend how income will be distributed, including pay out, withdrawals, and reinvestments; and
4. recommend or update investment strategies.

---

1 "Permanent Endowment and Planned Giving Ministry Committee," in *The Book of Discipline of The United Methodist Church: 2016* (Nashville, TN: Abingdon Press, 2016), ¶2534.

ORGANIZING AN ENDOWMENT MINISTRY: ROLES AND RESPONSIBILITIES (CONTINUED)

This team's work impacts the future sustainability of ministries by creating a long-term sustainable source of income funding specified activities. This draft agenda describes responsibilities of a new Endowment Committee.

Centering Prayer and Introduction of Members

Review Documents and Management Procedures

- Resolution—review responsibilities
- Spending Policy and Gifts Acceptance Policy
- Management system and recordkeeping

Review Investments/Fund Values

- Summary of endowment or invested assets
- Decision about Fund Manager

Create Marketing Plans and Resources

- How will we communicate this opportunity?
- How will we identify prospects?
- Brochure, newsletter, workshops, individual contacts, other

Develop Recordkeeping and Recognition Systems

- Establish system for recording gifts, donor information, and descriptions
- Donor Society, other options

Review of Assignments and Goals

Schedule Next Meeting and Go with Blessings!

Communication Responsibilities

The endowment team creates ongoing marketing strategies to keep this giving opportunity before members and donors. Examples include informational events, such as wills and estate planning seminars offered on a regular basis, and articles about endowment and planned giving gifts and distributions shared with all or selected members. A brochure, bulletin inserts, and promotional materials share the purpose of an endowment and encourage members and supporters to seek additional information. Depending on local circumstances, a campaign seeking endowment gifts from individuals and families or from all church members may be appropriate.

Communication activities may include

- creating primary educational brochures and resources including web links;
- developing a library of topical brochures;
- creating annual reports;
- maintaining originals of endowment documents, including gift acceptance policies;
- creating newsletter articles about donors and gift opportunities;
- providing general information to local estate planning professionals;
- determining method and frequency of distribution of materials, including email;
- preparing articles about donors and giving opportunities;
- determining who will respond to inquiries about the fund; and
- providing informational materials for responding to inquiries about the endowment fund.

Donor Cultivation: Identifying Prospects for Planned Gifts

The Endowment Committee creates a process for identifying and educating potential donors, including a follow-up system for prospects, a proposed timeline, and the type of follow-up to be used: letter, calls, or visits. In addition, consider cohort groups who may have planned giving interests: stages of life—persons caring for parents, professionals, preretirement, retirees; social groups—singles, young families, United Methodist Women, United Methodist Men, church school classes, and fellowship groups. The committee should maintain a list of potential donors, recommend who should be cultivated, and recruit those persons who should cultivate these relationships. The team also determines how gifts are acknowledged, typically based on gift size, and is responsible for donor recognition activities.

Below is a sample planned-giving prospect information form.

PLANNED-GIVING PROSPECT INFORMATION FORM

Prospect Name: ______________________________

Address: ______________________________

Phone/E-mail: ______________________________

History with Church: ______________________________

Giving History: ______________________________

Special Interests: ______________________________

Profession/Employer: ______________________________

Close Relations in Church: ______________________________

Best Person to Contact: ______________________________

Suggested by: ______________________________

Contact Date: ______________________________

____ sent brochure ____ phone contact ____ personal contact

Additional Comments:

Events

A launch event offers an opportunity to interpret the purpose of the fund and describe opportunities for making gifts. After the inaugural event, the committee makes regular reports to the governing body and interested groups such as the Trustees. The reports include the accomplishments of the ministry to date, an evaluation, and any recommendations for improvements in the ministry. The committee also

- develops lists of groups within the church to invite to special events;
- designs and hosts educational dialogues, presentations, workshops, or demonstrations;
- maintains a list of estate planning professionals in the community; and
- plans annual celebrations focusing on one endowment area each year.

Gift Processing

The Endowment Committee facilitates gift recognition and recordkeeping by

- ensuring all gifts get recorded by the financial secretary in a permanent location;
- keeping a permanent record that includes the donor's name, purpose, any restrictions, and when and how disbursed;
- notifying the financial secretary, who in turn notifies the designated person on the committee to supplement acknowledgments;
- sending acknowledgment letters, thank-you cards, and ongoing communication; and
- working with the treasurer to establish a recordkeeping and tracking system for transactions to endowment funds, including deposits, transfers, and withdrawals. This includes creating a report format for the treasurer to maintain a permanent record of the endowment ministry for reporting to the committee and Charge Conference.

Investment Responsibilities

The Endowment Committee oversees the investment of all assets described in the fund documentation, recommends investment policies, selects and monitors investment performance of the asset manager, and ensures an annual audit. The team monitors the endowment investment performance based on goals developed in consultation with appropriate advisors. If a fund manager other than a United Methodist investment manager is used, an investment strategy should ensure United Methodist guidelines for socially responsible and sustainable investing are followed and the investment goals of the committee are honored. The General Conference has assigned responsibility for United Methodist investment policy guidelines to the General Council on Finance and Administration (GCFA).[2] For assistance in formulating a local church investment strategy, refer to the Investment Guidelines

2 "Fiscal Responsibilities," in *The Discipline*, ¶806.12.

of the General Council on Finance and Administration of The United Methodist Church or your conference foundation.

Legal Responsibilities

The team reviews basic documents for conformity with applicable laws that apply to an endowment ministry and to ensure the documents represent the best interest of the church. They provide input to the Trustees and governing body about the acceptability of any gift, and represent the church with any attorney, CPA, or other estate planning professionals of a donor who is planning a specific gift.

Record retention responsibilities include identifying a permanent recordkeeping location and filing system. Adopted governing documents are filed with permanent records; if additional policies are adopted, they are also stored permanently with the related documents.[3]

Endowment Policy Sample

> **Disclaimer:** This sample is for educational purposes only. Drawn from work with United Methodist churches over the past two decades, the following sample offers typical policy content. Contact your United Methodist Foundation for more information because language is updated frequently. Always seek legal counsel to ensure compliance with appropriate statutory language and state regulations for financial policies regarding investments.

Endowment Fund and Committee Charter

Article 1: Purpose

The Endowment Fund and Committee of [name of mission] is established for the purpose of providing members and friends the opportunity to make charitable gifts to support our mission.

Article 2: Management and Stewardship

A. Endowment funds shall be administered by the Endowment Committee in accordance with the prevailing *Book of Discipline*.

---

3 Some portions of Organizing an Endowment Ministry are adapted from drafts proposed for the United Methodist Foundation of New England's "Planned Giving Handbook."

B. The funds managed by the committee shall be audited annually in accordance with the procedures prescribed in *The Book of Discipline.* The committee shall make reports to the Finance Committee twice a year on their investments.

C. The committee shall be accountable to the Church/Charge Conference for the proper application of the income of all funds as specified by the donors or endowment funds policy (see Article 3).

D. The committee shall act as the legal representative of the Church/Charge Conference, and all decisions or actions shall be in accordance with the vote of the Church/Charge Conference.

Article 3: Endowed Funds

A. Gifts and bequests received as endowments shall have the following investment objectives:

1) Conservation of principal for the effective maintenance of purchasing power
2) Regular income at a reasonable rate
3) Growth of income and principal over and above that necessary to offset increases in the cost of living (inflation)
4) Investment of assets in institutions, companies, corporations, or funds that make a positive contribution toward the realization of the goals outlined in the *Social Principles of The United Methodist Church*

B. The assets of the Endowment Fund shall be invested in one or more funds administered by [investment manager] or legal successor. When additions are made to the fund, the committee shall determine how the additions shall be allocated among the subfunds, and the committee may change the allocation from time to time.

C. The committee shall maintain a permanent record of the specific purpose of each endowment. The committee may combine into a single account all gifts having the same restrictions on the use of income and may maintain a single account for all gifts not having any restriction on the use of income. The committee shall keep appropriate permanent records of the identity of donors of bequests and special gifts, and of any persons for whom a gift is made.

D. Use of any investment agency other than a United Methodist investment manager shall be approved by the governing board. If any assets are transferred for investment with another agency, the committee shall, in consultation with the Church/Charge Conference, establish policies to ensure that investments will make a positive contribution toward the realization of the goals outlined in the *Social Principles of The United Methodist Church.*

E. If the laws of the state permit expenditure of the principal of restricted endowments, then in addition to any approval for such action required by state law, approval must be obtained from the Church/Charge Conference by a two-thirds vote of the members present and voting at a meeting duly called for such purpose at which a quorum is present.

F. Having in mind that overly detailed restrictions on purposes may be impractical to administer, prospective donors shall be encouraged to add their gifts to consolidated accounts, permitting the use of the income for broadly defined programs of the church including, but not limited to, the following examples:

- *Endowment Fund*: A fund in which principal is protected and disbursements are limited to income and growth as appropriate to maintain the fund value, after the fund reaches a value of $100,000. When distributions begin, funds will support mission or maintenance projects.
- *Music and Worship Fund*: Earning for this fund may be used for investments that ensure the professional maintenance of our musical instruments or expand the instruments available for ministry and worship.
- *Additional accounts* may be established from time to time by the committee, and accounts for more restricted purposes may be established by the committee with the consent of the Church/Charge Conference. The Church/Charge Conference may from time to time

specify the minimum amount that may be allocated to any account restricted as to income.

Article 4: Liability of Trustees and Members of the Committee

No member of the committee shall be liable for any investment made in any fund administered by an outside organization.

Article 5: Merger, Consolidation, or Dissolution

If at any time [name of mission] is lawfully merged or consolidated, all the provisions hereof in respect to the fund shall be deemed to have been made on behalf of the merged or consolidated entity, which shall be obligated to administer the same in all respects and in accordance with the terms thereto. If [name of mission] should ever be dissolved without any lawful successor thereof, this document shall empower [name of successor] to continue distribution of income while maintaining the preservation of endowment principal and authorizing a successor institution to assume the powers afforded to [name of mission]. The fund shall at that time include both principal and interest to date.

Article 6: Amendments

The provisions of Articles 1 and 5 shall constitute a contract between [name of mission] and the respective donors. Any amendment of Article 1 shall apply only to gifts made after the effective date of the amendment.

Subject to the foregoing, this charter may be amended by a two-thirds vote of the members present and voting at a Church/Charge conference duly called for such purpose. All proposed amendments must conform to the current version of *The Book of Discipline of The United Methodist Church*.

The Undersigned certify that this charter was adopted or amended by a vote of: ______ FOR ______ AGAINST ______ ABSTAINED

At a duly called meeting of the Charge Conference of [name and address of mission] held at [location] on [date] (notice of the proposed action having been given in the call of the meeting).

Recording Secretary: ______________________________

Pastor: ______________________________

District Superintendent: ______________________________

APPENDIX D
FINANCE POLICIES

These sample policies define operational and financial procedures that should be reviewed annually. They are offered as a resource for developing local policies created with your mission context and structure in mind.[1]

Operations and Financial Management Policies

I. Operating Funds (Definitions)

Operating/Annual Budget: The Annual Budget is the church's yearly operations spending plan prepared by the Finance Committee in consultation with the Church Council and approved by the Charge Conference or Church Conference. The annual budget includes all work area budgets, the Trustees' budget, and all staff budgets. Once approved, it authorizes disbursement of funds up to the levels indicated. All operations payments are made by the treasurer (or designated staff person).

In and Out Accounts: These are a form of designated funds. In and out accounts are holding accounts established to receive, hold, and manage revenue received for a specific purpose or activity. Since they represent designated monies, each will be controlled by a designated account manager.

Invested Funds: The church may choose to invest available funds to maximize stewardship of resources. The Trustees are responsible for overseeing

---

1 Adapted from work by William Miller and other local church financial leaders. See also https://www.flumc.org/financialservices for an example of online resources becoming available through annual conferences.

and managing invested funds unless delegated to an Endowment or Investment Committee. Finance Committee consultation is recommended before reporting to the Church Council (governing body). Endowment funds are governed by an adopted endowment policy.

Other Funds/Income: Other off-budget income or expenses shall be authorized by the Church Council after review and recommendations by the Finance Committee. The Trustees are responsible for reviewing all planned gifts, bequests, or donor-restricted gifts. Consultation with finance leadership is recommended before reporting recommendations on acceptance or renegotiation with the donor. All gift recommendations require approval by the Charge Conference. All funds are subject to the annual audit.

II. Managing the Annual Budget

Preparing the Annual Budget: The annual budget is developed by the Finance Committee in consultation with ministry areas and approved by the Church Council. The Finance Committee is responsible for generating sufficient funds for the envisioned ministry and reporting recommendations to the Church Council.

The Finance Committee will develop a schedule for budget requests from committees and ministry areas. This initial input will form a first draft of the new spending plan. The Finance Committee may consult with committees or ministry areas (excluding PPRC/SPRC) to review or revise their request prior to Church Council discussion. This dialogue ensures all activities are represented in the budget development process and a realistic budget proposal is presented.

The financial secretary, in consultation with the Finance Committee, will prepare an income estimate for the budget year based on the current and recent past years' activities. This estimate, compared to the draft budget, will inform the various steps necessary to proceed toward developing a balanced budget.

If a draft budget proposal would require more funds than may be expected to be available, a joint meeting of the Finance Committee and the Church Council will be held to review alternatives and select a course of action. This may include such things as assessing revenue, prioritizing requirements, and deferring expenditures as possible ways to bring the budget in line with expected available funds. The goal is an essentially balanced budget with a fully funded spending plan using either anticipated revenues or disbursement of liquid undesignated assets.

Approving the Budget/Spending Plan: All work areas and other activities represented in the budget may review the draft budget. Approval of this draft budget will precede preparation of the final budget to be presented for approval.

A Charge Conference will be held to present the proposed budget for approval. The finance chairperson will present the budget and answer any questions prior to calling for the vote. The approved budget will be distributed to all work area and other activity managers.

The approved budget includes a total amount for each work area and other line items as required by the *Book of Discipline* or regional conference. Subaccounts have been created for planning and reporting purposes only.

Managing the Budget/Spending Plan: Managing the approved budget and operating within the funding authorized is managed by leadership of each of the areas funded in the budget, as well as the Finance Committee, which includes the treasurer and the financial secretary. Work area managers and other activity managers are responsible for monitoring their expenditures. The treasurer will provide periodic reports to each manager to provide current information on spending to date.

The Finance Committee will review current and year-to-date income and spending at least quarterly based on the reports provided by the treasurer and financial secretary. If adjustments are needed, the Finance Committee will communicate their findings and recommend possible courses of action to the Church Council.

III. Accounts

Structure of Internal Accounting System: Two master accounts, (1) a permanent expense account and (2) a revolving (or in and out) account, will be established for each work area and other activities (e.g., Trustees and Staff Parish Relations Committee/Pastor Parish Relations Committee). The master accounts for each area will be an ongoing account, as it is a holding account for all of that area's subaccounts.

Establishing New Accounts: To accommodate the diverse activities within each work area, subaccounts may be established. All new accounts shall be approved by the Church Council upon recommendation from the Finance Committee. Each will be assigned to a work area or other activity chairperson for management and control.

Managing Accounts: Each work area is responsible for its assigned accounts. These include requesting a new account for a new activity, monitoring all income to the account, requesting payments from the appropriate account, and closing the account and transferring remaining funds to an appropriate account when the account is no longer needed. The treasurer will disburse appropriate expenses from in and out account revenues before committee budget resources and will maintain a record of income and expenditures for each account, providing periodic status information to account managers. The Finance Committee will monitor the overall structure to ensure accounts are opened, managed, appropriately billed, and closed when no longer needed.

IV. Internal Controls

Separation of Duties: The treasurer, financial secretary, and Finance Committee chair shall not be the same person or from the same family or household.

Budget: The church shall have a budget. Financial status and expenses should be compared to the budget on a monthly or quarterly basis. Variances from the budget will be reviewed to identify any adjustments needed.

Bank Accounts: All operating checking and savings accounts shall be under control of the treasurer. Separate checking accounts, other than United Methodist Women ministries, for church activities are discouraged. Investment accounts statements are received by the treasurer and activity reported monthly or quarterly.

Authorizing Signatures: Annually, the Church Council shall approve the signatories on all church accounts.

Payroll: Quarterly, the finance chair should inquire of the treasurer at a meeting whether all payroll taxes have been timely paid to state and federal authorities.

Audit: The Church Council should require and review an annual audit of church finances by a person other than the treasurer, financial secretary, finance chairperson, or counters.

Recordkeeping: All financial records should be retained in accordance with the following record-retention policy.[2]

Item	Retention
Bank statements and reconciliations	7 years
Canceled checks for standard transactions	7 years
Invoices from vendors	7 years
W-2 or 1099 forms	7 years
Housing allowance forms	7 years
Business correspondence	3 years
Employee personnel records (after termination)	3 years

V. Purchasing Procedures

Types of Purchases: These procedures cover purchases made to support all church programs, facilities, staff, hard goods, and services. Contingencies and emergencies are also covered.

Authorization: The annual budget provides the basic authorization to purchase goods and services to support church activities. In and out accounts provide authorization to use funds as provided in the description of the account. Purchases that are clearly outside the scope of the budget or exceed authorized funding levels should be referred to the Finance Committee for review and recommendation to the Council for resolution. Receipts and appropriate documentation are required.

2 Adapted from General Council on Finance and Administration (GCFA) website http://s3.amazonaws.com/gcah.org/Resources/Guidelines_Publications/ConfRetSched.2013.pdf, 28–31.

Purchase: Purchases may be made by any congregational member authorized by the manager of an appropriate budget element or in and out account. Valid purchases are those that support a recognized church activity. Payment Request Forms are available in the office or from the treasurer. Whenever possible, vendors should be paid directly by the church rather than through members' personal funds.

Office purchases will normally be made or managed by the administrative assistant.

The Trustees will normally make purchases or acquire services to support the operation of the church and the parsonage. Purchases will be approved by the work area or other activity manager, who will also provide payment instructions to the treasurer. Purchases greater than $500, or reimbursements being paid to and authorized by the work area manager, require a second authorizing signature on the Payment Request Form. The second authorizing signature may be another member of the work area, Council chair, Finance chair, or pastor.

Payment: Purchases will generally be paid for by the treasurer based on a request from the purchaser or appropriate fund or budget area manager. Whenever possible, vendors should be paid directly by the church rather than through members' personal funds. When purchases are paid for by the purchaser, a request for reimbursement will be presented to the treasurer together with a receipt and identification of the budget element or in and out account to charge.

Accounting: The treasurer is the keeper of the church financial books. To do this, work area and other activity leaders must keep the treasurer up to date on purchases made and bills expected to be received. This notification should also include funding information, including the budget element or in and out account used to pay a bill or provide reimbursement for a purchase. The treasurer will disburse appropriate in and out accounts first and may adjust account assignments if needed.

VI. Managing Receipts and Deposits

Counters: Counters are responsible for counting all receipts on a weekly basis and preparing all cash, checks, and currency for deposit. Two unrelated counters are assigned the tasks, with one recording the receipts to appropriate accounts and donor records and the other counting receipts in preparation for deposit. The recorded value must equal the total deposit. The deposit slip and deposit are placed in a bank deposit bag and locked. A copy of the deposit slip is given to the treasurer for recordkeeping and comparison to the bank statement.

Financial Secretary: Among other duties, the financial secretary is responsible for reconciling the counters' deposit report with appropriate accounts and donor records. Additional breakdown and appropriation of these recorded receipts may include designations to in and out categories.

Account Reconciliation: Bank account reconciliations should be performed monthly and reviewed by the Finance Committee chair at least quarterly. This review includes an examination of checks issued to ensure proper church purposes. Copies or images of all cancelled checks will be retained with the bank statements.

VII. Reimbursement Accounts

Accountable Reimbursement Policy *(to be adopted annually upon SPRC presentation)*

The [name of mission] recognizes that certain expenses of ministry paid by the pastor/staff person are part of the ordinary and necessary costs of ministry. Accordingly, we hereby establish an accountable reimbursement policy to defray them directly. The reimbursement account shall be an annual line item in the church budget. It shall be in addition to the pastor's annual salary and housing.

The following requirements for the policy are binding upon the church and upon its pastor/staff. Accordingly, an accountable reimbursement policy is established, pursuant to IRS regulations and upon the following terms and conditions:

1. The pastor/staff person shall be reimbursed from the reimbursement account for ordinary, necessary, and reasonable business expenses incurred in the conduct of the ministry for, and on behalf of, the church. The following expenses are budgeted in this accountable reimbursement policy, as suggested for the work needs of the pastor/staff person, and are suggested items

for inclusion in this accountable reimbursement policy. To allow for the pastor's/staff person's spending discretion, only the total amount is necessary to be reported as a line item in the Charge Conference–approved budget.

A. Automobile (standard federal mileage rate), parking, and tolls, excluding travel to church

B. Office supplies and postage

C. Office equipment, computer, and software

D. Books, subscriptions, and periodicals such as professional journals

E. Professional dues

F. Religious materials, vestments, and business gifts

G. Continuing education and seminars, as approved by the PPR/SPRC

H. Entertainment required for church business

I. Travel fares, lodging, and meals while on business for the church

2. The Staff/Pastor Parish Relations Committee (PPR/SPRC) chairperson, payroll person, or treasurer must be given an adequate accounting within sixty days after the expense is paid or incurred. The adequate accounting shall include, but not be limited to, a statement of expense, account-book diary or other similar record showing the amount, date, place, business purpose, and business relationship involved. Such documentation shall include receipts for all items of $75 or more.

Appropriate documents, cash receipts, canceled checks, credit card sales slips, and contemporaneous records for non-receipt expenses less than $75, must be attached to each expense report. A log of total miles per day and enumeration of their general purpose shall suffice to substantiate automobile mileage, but under no circumstances will commuting mileage between the pastor's home and church office be reimbursed. Copies of the documentary evidence and expense report shall be retained by both the pastor and the church.

The PPR/SPRC chairperson or treasurer shall be authorized to approve the expense. The SPRC chairperson or treasurer shall exercise personal discretion regarding the adequacy of the substantiation and the appropriateness of any reimbursement. Questions arising in these areas will be resolved by the PPR/SPRC chairperson, subject to the review and approval of the SPRC or Finance Committee.

3. It is the intention of this policy that reimbursements will be paid after the expense has been incurred. However, should circumstances require payment of an advance for any particular anticipated expense, the pastor must account for the expense as described above and return any excess reimbursement within 120 days after the expense is paid or incurred. Any excess advance must be returned to the church before any additional advances are provided to the pastor.

4. Budgeted amounts not spent must not be paid as a salary bonus or other personal compensation. If such payments are made, the entire amount of the accountable reimbursement policy account will be taxable income to the pastor/staff person. The church will be required by law to report that amount as part of the pastor's compensation. Any unspent balances remain at the discretion of the Finance Committee.

5. It is understood by the various parties that all elements of this resolution must be carefully followed to prevent the church from being required by regulation to include all reimbursements as income on the pastor's Form W-2. The primary responsibility in this regard resides with the pastor to report and adequately account for his or her expenses to the PPR/SPRC chairperson and treasurer.

APPENDIX E

GIFT ACCEPTANCE POLICY SAMPLE

Disclaimer to Donors and Policy Adopters: Review and revise these policies as needed. A local attorney and/or real estate agent should review the terminology and basic recommendations before adoption.[1]

[Name of mission] has adopted the following policy regarding gifts that may be considered for acceptance to further our mission work. The purpose of this Gift Acceptance Policy is to describe the types of gifts accepted and the review process prior to acceptance. Where an Endowment Committee does not exist, The Board of Trustees is instructed by the Charge Conference to receive and distribute gifts received under the Gift Acceptance Policy.

Unrestricted cash gifts will be accepted and acknowledged through the normal accounting procedures of [name of mission].

Restricted gifts will be reviewed prior to acceptance and may require renegotiation with the donor.

Gifts may be deposited in Memorial or Endowment Funds. The Trustees or Endowment Committee are responsible for reviewing memorials and endowment gifts and establishing appropriate recognition procedures.

Receipt of non-cash gifts will be the responsibility of the Trustees or Endowment Committee. The committee reserves the right to return or refuse

---

1 Other samples available at https://gbod-assets.s3.amazonaws.com/legacy/kintera-files/stewardship/SAMPLE-GIFT-ACCEPTANCE-POLICY-july2014.pdf.

any gift determined to be unacceptable because of value, marketability, or any other reason deemed problematic.

All non-cash gifts, except for real estate, will be immediately liquidated. Gifts of stock, various kinds of securities, insurance products, automobiles, animals, jewelry, and other items of value must be unencumbered and given outright. If the gift is deemed acceptable, the gifts will immediately be sold in a manner deemed most appropriate by the Trustees or Endowment Committee.

All gifts of real estate must be given with an appropriate title search, environmental evaluation, survey, and appraisal. All costs of transferring, known and discovered during transfer, will be borne by the donor. Gifts of real estate must be unencumbered with liens, litigation, or any other potential liability. Before the title is accepted, the Trustees and Endowment Committee reserve the right to not accept the gift.

All non-cash gifts will be acknowledged in a dated letter from the chairperson of the Trustees or Endowment Committee, which will include a description of the gift and appropriate substantiation language. There will be no appraisal, acknowledgment of appraisal, or determination of value offered in the acknowledgment process. The donor has sole responsibility to the Internal Revenue Service for identifying the value of any non-cash gift.

Any questions regarding this policy should be referred to the chairperson of the Trustees or Endowment Committee.

APPENDIX F

MEMORIAL FUND POLICY SAMPLE

Disclaimer: This sample offers suggestions for managing and stewarding gifts to a designated fund in honor of persons or life events, known as a Memorial Fund.

Purpose: This policy establishes a Memorial Fund at [Ministry Name] to receive and steward these designated gifts.

Funding: Gifts to the [Church Name] Memorial Fund are given in recognition of a person's life, often at the time of a funeral, or to celebrate a special event, such as birthday, graduation, wedding, or other accomplishment. Gifts are cash only. Other in-kind gifts or gifts of assets shall be referred to the Endowment Fund Committee/Trustees for review and gift acceptance procedures.

Distributions: When memorial gifts are received following the death of a member or constituent, family members may be invited to suggest possible uses for funds donated. Within six months of the funeral, funds available for the suggested purpose shall be reviewed. If the gift amount is less than the cost of the suggested item, the family will be contacted by the Finance Committee and given the option of covering the additional cost or suggesting another item. If sufficient funds are available, the surplus funds shall be released to the Finance Committee for alternative use. Consultation with a Memorial Gifts Committee, if it exists, will occur.

Stewardship: Memorial gifts shall be dispersed within twenty-four months of receipt, using one or a combination of any of the following options:

(1) Purchasing a specific item for the church or any of its ministries, (2) contributing to a church project or budgeted expense, or (3) depositing all or some of the gift into an endowment.

Any questions or concerns should be directed to the Finance Committee.

Date Adopted: ____________________

APPENDIX G

PASTOR'S DISCRETIONARY FUND POLICY SAMPLE

Disclaimer: This sample offers suggestions for funding, managing, and documenting funds used for emergency financial support at the discretion of pastoral leadership. Policies and procedures provide important guidance and protection while allowing confidential financial support. Accounts or payments should never be made in the name of the pastor.

Purpose: This policy defines management responsibilities to ensure the safety of resources and pastors provided with a Pastor's Discretionary Fund at [name of mission]. Any concerns or questions shall be directed to the [governing body, personnel, or finance leadership].

Funding: The Pastor's Discretionary Fund is funded by [description of how funds are designated or raised]. The pastor shall submit requests for discretionary funds to the treasurer. The treasurer shall remit funds to the pastor as indicated on the request voucher. The approved limit on advances from the Discretionary Fund is [specify amount].

Distributions: The pastor is encouraged to use funds for goods and services, rather than cash assistance (for example, bus tickets or taxi fare, groceries, or hotel bill payment).

Records: The pastor is responsible for documenting distribution of the fund. All records are confidential and held by the pastor. The church acknowledges that the pastor is authorized to distribute these funds at his or her discretion and is not required to provide any details regarding who receives assistance. The church may request general information regarding types of assistance (food, transportation) given to assess the changing needs of the community.

Reporting: The treasurer shall report the beginning and end-of-year balance of the Discretionary Fund in the annual report and for the annual audit.

Date Adopted ______________ By ______________________________

Pastor's Signature ______________________________ Date __________

Treasurer's Signature ______________________________ Date __________

Finance Chairperson's Signature ____________________ Date __________

APPENDIX H

SAFE SANCTUARY AND LIMITED ACCESS POLICY SAMPLES

Disclaimer: The legal and financial costs for organizations without policies addressing safety for all persons can be catastrophic. These samples are for general guideline use only; some sections may not apply to your specific setting. Your policies should specifically address your context and community safety issues and the local laws regarding protection from harm, especially for minors and vulnerable populations.

Safe Sanctuary Policy Sample[1]

Purpose

The purpose of this policy is to demonstrate our absolute and unwavering commitment to the physical safety and spiritual growth of our children and youth. We strive to ensure [name of mission] is a safe sanctuary where children, youth, and vulnerable adults are nurtured, confirmed, and strengthened in their faith journeys. It includes policies and procedures for all who use our facilities and work with children, youth, or vulnerable persons. It is our intention to always provide a safe and supervised environment wherever our ministries may take place. We want to bring light to the issue of physical or emotional abuse so that there is an open atmosphere around this issue.

---

1 Adapted from local church and conference samples created using denominational resources. Always seek local legal counsel for compliance with local and state laws. Additional samples located at https://www.umcdiscipleship.org/resources/safe-sanctuaries-general-guidelines-starter-documents.

Guidelines

1. No person will be left solely in charge of children or youth in any situation. A volunteer or paid staff member must be at least five years older than the youth they are supervising.
2. Classrooms must be accessible to viewing at all times. Windows to classrooms will be not be blocked by objects or curtains.
3. Doors should be kept open at all times during one-on-one counseling or while advising youth.
4. Two adults should be present at all programs involving children and youth. A "floater" who moves from room to room will constitute a second adult; however, the floater must be in the building during the program hours.
5. Bathroom doors will remain open. Individual stall doors will be closed when in use.
6. All adults must complete a self-assessment form and a Criminal Offender Record Information (CORI) check. Church leaders will be responsible for the cost of the CORI test. Outside groups, such as Scouting programs, will be responsible for the cost of the CORI test for their leaders.
7. Teachers will always accompany a child who goes outside of the classroom.
8. Children in third grade or younger must be accompanied by a parent or guardian to their classrooms or in-church event location. Parents/guardians must stay with children until both supervisory adults are present. Parents/guardians must pick up children third grade or younger from their classroom or in-church location.
9. If an adult unfamiliar to the adult supervisor has permission to pick up a child, permission must be in writing and signed by the parent or guardian.
10. No child should be outside the building without an adult.
11. No child should be in the kitchen area unless they are with a parent or guardian.
12. Youth Group parents will complete an annual transportation and per-

mission slip. Long-distance events will have a separate permission form. All overnight youth events must have a minimum of two adult chaperones; one must be male, and one must be female. Youth under the age of eighteen are encouraged to have a medical release form on file with the Youth Group leaders.

Church Commitments

1. We will offer two opportunities each year for parishioners and families to learn the facts about child-abuse prevention and about our Safe Sanctuary.
2. We will make resources available in our library to educate parishioners and families about child-abuse prevention.
3. We will offer a CPR and first aid class for all of our volunteers, including Scout leaders and teachers.
4. The Education Committee will review tasks 1–9, pp. 44–49, *Safe Sanctuaries: Reducing the Risk of Child Abuse in the Church,* recommending adjustments to this policy to the Staff Parish Relations Committee.
5. When an incident of child abuse occurs, we will respond according to the following procedure:
   a. Reports of child abuse can be made to [name of the designee of the Staff Parish Relations Committe], pastor, or Christian Education director. If the report comes from someone other than a parent or guardian and does not involve a parent or guardian, the child's parents or guardians will be notified immediately. Emergency care if necessary will be provided in consultation with the parents or guardians. For the person receiving the report, the physical and emotional health of the child is of critical importance. The question of reporting to the police will be raised with the family. An incident report will be completed.
   b. Upon receipt of a report, the person receiving the report will call a meeting of the Review Committee (Staff Parish designee, senior pastor, and Christian Education director) within one week. They will ensure that the accused perpetrator will no longer have unsupervised

contact with children until the accusation is resolved. Minutes of the review meeting will be kept in a confidential file.

c. If the report is of sexual abuse, the senior pastor will notify [state mandated report recipient]. If the senior pastor is named as an enabler or perpetrator, then the designee of the Staff Parish Relations Committee will notify the [state mandated report recipient].

d. After a meeting of the Review Committee, the person receiving the initial report will contact the victim and/or family and share the action that the church will be taking. It is assumed that the Review Committee meeting will result in some action. If not already reported and the Review Committee feels strongly about the need for reporting to the legal authorities, the family will be encouraged to file a criminal report.

e. The designee of the Staff Parish Relations Committee will serve as the designated person to deal with the press.

f. Documentation of these actions will be maintained in a confidential file.

g. Pastoral care will be provided for the child and family as long as necessary. This policy suggests that there is a beginning and an end to an incident of child abuse; however, we recognize that an end for the child and family may be in the distant future.

h. Pastoral care will also be provided to the accused perpetrator and family by the senior pastor or by a neighboring pastor, if necessary.

Volunteer Application Form Sample

Name: ____

Address: ____

City, State and Zip Code: ______________________________

Home and Business Phone: _____________________________

Other name(s), if any, by which I have been known: ____________

Previous volunteer work including dates, type of work, and reference with contact information:

Personal Reference: ______________________ Telephone: ___________

Personal Statement by Name: __________________ Date: ___________

1. I have never been found guilty, or pleaded guilty or no contest, to a criminal charge.

   True _____ Not True _____

2. No civil lawsuit alleging actual or attempted sexual discrimination, harassment, exploitation, or misconduct; physical abuse; child abuse; or financial misconduct has ever resulted in a judgment being entered against me, been settled out of court, or been dismissed because the statute of limitations has expired.

   True _____ Not True _____

3. I have never terminated my employment or service in a volunteer position or had my employment or authorization to hold a volunteer position terminated, for reasons relating to allegations of actual or attempted sexual discrimination, exploitation, or misconduct; physical abuse; child abuse; or financial misconduct.

   True _____ Not True _____

If answering "not true" to any of the above, please attach a short explanation of the charge, indicating the date, nature, and place of the incident leading to the charge, where the charge was filed, and the precise disposition of the charge or lawsuit.

Limited Access Policy Samples

Disclaimer: When parties wish to establish a limited access policy, these three samples suggest some possible covenant language.[2] All parties must agree fully, and any violations void any agreements. All such agreements are voluntary and will be disclosed to the faith community. These policies do not guarantee safety and should be entered into with careful consideration and

2 Samples adapted from work by New England Conference Response Team, 2017. Used with permission. Consultation with local legal consultation is expected before use in other settings.

oversight. These polices do not provide legal or liability protection should further incidents occur.

Example 1. Behavioral Covenant

[Name of Mission] Limited Access Covenant with [Name of Individual]

The [name of mission] affirms the dignity and worth of all persons. We are committed to being a Christian community with "open hearts, open minds, and open doors." All persons in our church must have confidence and assurance that we are committed to preserving the church as a holy place of safety and protection for all.

We have determined that you were involved in recent incidents of unwanted or unacceptable behavior. This pattern of inappropriate behavior is a violation of our community's covenant. We must ensure the physical and emotional safety of those with whom you come in contact in our congregation. We welcome you to our congregation and our membership, and we need to limit certain aspects of your participation to protect you from future accusations and to ensure the safety of others. The purpose of the following guidelines is to reduce the risk to both you and the parishioners of any accusations or incidents causing harm. We believe it is in everyone's best interest to limit your contact, as defined below, with children, adults, or any vulnerable persons on congregational property or at congregation-sponsored events.

Within the following guidelines, the congregation welcomes your participation in [name of church]. We invite you to agree to the following:

1. I will not volunteer or agree to lead, chaperone, or participate in events for children and youth, including such things as Sunday school classes, children's time during worship, Youth Group events, nursery care, Vacation Bible School, activities during intergenerational events, and driving or otherwise transporting children, youth, or other vulnerable persons.
2. Except for handshakes, I will refrain from all physical contact, including hugging, with parishioners.
3. I will not come into the church building during regular office hours [list church's office hours] without the pastor's and the office or program administrator's prior consent.
4. I will submit to a background check by completing and returning the

attached consent form, in person, to either the pastor or the Safe Sanctuary Team chair.

I have reviewed this covenant and agree to abide by its provisions.
I understand that this covenant will remain in effect for an indefinite period of time.

Signature	Print Name	Date
Pastor		
Lay Leader		
Safe Sanctuary Team Chair		

Example 2. Conditional Attendance Covenant (criminal record possessor)

[Name of Mission] Limited Access Covenant with [Name of Individual]

[Name of mission] affirms the dignity and worth of all persons. We are committed to protecting and keeping our community of faith open to those who need to worship with us, especially in times of serious personal trouble. However, based on your prior criminal conviction, we need to restrict your contact with children and youth in our congregation. The following guidelines will reduce the risk, to both you and them, of an incident or accusation. We welcome you to our congregation and our membership, and your participation will be limited for the sake of the safety of our children, youth, or other vulnerable persons and to help protect you from any unwarranted accusations.

Within these guidelines, the congregation welcomes your participation in any adult worship services, coffee hour, committee meetings, adult education, and adult social events.

By signing this covenant, you acknowledge that you understand you will not be allowed to volunteer or chaperone events for children or adolescents, including children's religious education classes, talks with children or adolescents during worship services, youth group, children's and adolescents' activities during intergenerational events, or transporting children or young people. Do not volunteer or agree to be involved in any events for children and youth. Remain in the presence of adults whenever children are present.

Acknowledgment: I have reviewed this covenant and agree to abide by its provisions. I agree that if I violate this agreement in any way, I will be denied access to future church functions and church property. I understand that this agreement will be reviewed regularly, possibly every six months, and will remain in effect for an indefinite time period. Continuation of this covenant may be dependent upon my continuing participation in treatment and/or recovery program. The individual terms of this covenant may be changed by [name of church] at any time for any reason deemed appropriate by committee members.

________________	________________	________
Signature	Print Name	Date
________________	________________	________
Witness		
________________	________________	________
Witness		

Example 3. Limitations for Registered Sex Offenders

[Name of Mission] Limited Access Covenant with [Name of Individual]

[Name of mission] affirms the dignity and worth of all persons. We are committed to be a Christian community with "open hearts, open minds, and open doors." Based on your status as a registered sex offender, we need to protect you and ensure the safety of those in our congregation with whom you come in contact. The following guidelines will reduce the risk of an accusation or incident to both you and parishioners. We welcome you to our congregation and our membership, yet we need to limit your participation so that you will not be subject to future unwarranted accusations and for the safety of our church people, particularly children and youth.

Within the following guidelines, the congregation values you and welcomes your participation in [name of church]. We need you to avoid contact with children, youth, and any other vulnerable persons on congregational property or at congregation-sponsored events.

We expect you to agree to the following:

1. For my protection I will not have any physical or verbal contact with any person under the age of eighteen. If a person under eighteen years old initiates verbal contact, the conversation will remain brief and concise. If a person under eighteen years of age initiates physical contact, I will refuse and step away.
2. I will not enter the Sunday school wing. I will remain in the fellowship hall, kitchen, or sanctuary only and at all times.
3. If I need to visit the restroom, I will have a member of the SPRC or individual appointed by the pastor to check that the restroom is clear before I enter.
4. I will not have a key to any church building. If I now have a key to the building, I must return it to the pastor.
5. I will periodically discuss this covenant when requested by the pastor.
6. I will limit my attendance to Sunday service and church suppers. If I decide to attend another event, I will gain permission from the pastor before attending.
7. If I relocate my membership, [name of church] will support me in disclosing to the new church's leadership.

I accept the congregation will be told of my circumstances in order to protect me and for them to protect the children, young people, and other vulnerable persons for whom they care. I have reviewed this covenant and agree to abide by its provisions. I understand and agree that if I violate this agreement, the church will take action as outlined in the current version of the *Book of Discipline* (¶ 2702) and our Conference Misconduct Policy.

I understand that this covenant will be periodically reviewed and will remain in effect for an indefinite time period.

____________________ ____________________ __________

Signature Print Name Date

____________________ ____________________ __________

Pastor

____________________ ____________________ __________

Staff Parish Relations Chair

APPENDIX I

STEWARDSHIP COMMITTEE START-UP

Agenda Template for a New Stewardship Team[1]

First Meeting

1. Open with prayer and introduction of members.
2. Identify the leadership roles of Chair and Secretary.
3. Create a meeting calendar for the year; the number of meetings will determine the amount of work achievable.
4. Dialogue about what *stewardship* means and why it is a way of life.
5. Begin to identify a multiyear stewardship plan, setting priorities for the current year, and what to address in future years.
6. Create a plan for engaging in stewardship formation and dialogue each meeting. Assign responsibility for the learning elements of each meeting, and identify resources available for study by the group.
7. Invite questions and further dialogue or input.
8. Announce next meeting date, offer affirmation and thanksgiving, and adjourn.

---

1 Adapted from "Stewardship Committee—Meeting Outline," in *Stewardship Sourcebook* (New Canaan, CT: Parish Publishing Inc. LLC, 2014), 38–39; www.parishpublishing.org. Used with permission.

Second Meeting

1. Begin with prayer and welcome; check in on members' lives.
2. Do stewardship formation or study, exercise.
3. Review and finalize current year plan, and future year recommendations, and create goals for accomplishing current year plans.
4. Discuss and assign tasks for current year's goals: who, when, how.
5. Review assignments and tasks to ensure clarity and commitment.
6. Invite questions and further dialogue or input.
7. Confirm leadership for next meeting's stewardship formation exercise.
8. Announce next meeting date, offer affirmation, and adjourn.

Third and Future Meetings

1. Begin with prayer and welcome; check in on members' lives.
2. Do stewardship formation or study, exercise, sharing, and review.
3. Provide ongoing updates on tasks and progress, goals and next steps, accomplishments, witnesses, and congregational education and resources.
4. Invite questions and further dialogue or input.
5. Confirm leadership for next meeting's stewardship formation exercise.
6. Announce next meeting date, offer affirmation, and adjourn.

APPENDIX J
WORKSHEETS

WORKSHEET 1. Biblical Stewardship

Prayerfully explore the beliefs about generosity expressed by these biblical principles described in chapter 1. Consider how they are expressed or embodied in your life and profession.

Reflection: Everything Is a Gift

1. Briefly describe God's gifts in your life.
2. Do you consider your income *mine* or *God's gift* to you?
3. Do your mission's financial leaders talk about *our* budget or *God's* budget?
4. What difference does it make to shift from *mine* or *ours* to *God's*? [1]
5. Does this first tenet cause you to smile?
6. Why does this awareness of God as the giver need to occur first?

Reflection: We Are Chosen as Stewards

1. Describe an early experience of being chosen. What happens when we are chosen? When we realize God has chosen us?
2. What barriers prevent us from seeing all persons as chosen by God?
3. What are the costs or responsibilities of chosen stewards?
4. When did you last set personal financial goals or assess your saving, retirement, or legacy planning?
5. Are your financial goals and visions aligned with caring for God's creation and all people?

---

1 Credited to Rev. Anne Robertson, Executive Director, Massachusetts Bible Society, Boston, MA, first used in 1996. Used with permission.

6. When were your church finances last audited and financial procedures reviewed?
7. Name three ways you or your church fulfill the responsibilities of a steward chosen by God.

Reflection: God's Preference for the Poor

1. Share your personal call or passion for mission. How do you want to change the world?
2. How does your church invite people to identify their call and ministry commitments?
3. Are people in your congregation more likely to send a financial gift or to visit a mission site?
4. What are the greatest needs in your community or your global connections?

Reflection: Today Matters

1. Please share about your personal passion for mission.
2. Describe an opportunity you or someone you know missed because they didn't take action, or an action you are going to take to create a new opportunity.
3. Share a story about saving and debt. What needs to change now? When will you do it?
4. What are your church's values about saving and debt? What needs to change? Who will do it?
5. How are your personal values similar or different from your congregation?
6. How can you promote planned giving to support future missions?

Missional Reflection

1. Look for evidence of these biblical generosity principles in your worship services, in your meetings and programs, in your outreach and missions, and in your educational activities for all ages. Record your observations and share with other leaders.
2. Brainstorm new ways to express these beliefs in worship, in education, in communications with current members, with newcomers, with lapsed members, and with your community. Record your ideas and share with other leaders.
3. Explore how these beliefs and values inform your missional stewardship of money. What feels strong and evident in your activities? What deserves more attention? Record and share your responses with appropriate groups and leaders.

WORKSHEET 2. Personal Stewardship

After recording your personal responses, share this worksheet with a friend or family member. Personal finance professionals consistently urge us to make life decisions today so that—rather than causing problems and conflicts—we bless others by our stewardship of God's gifts. Prayerfully consider and record your responses to this financial stewardship self-assessment.

1. Select the option that best matches your confidence about managing your personal finances.

   ______ Very confident

   ______ Confident, but could do better or would like help

   ______ Not confident, need help

2. My personal finances are

   ______ a practical responsibility.

   ______ a task I endure.

   ______ an aspect of my spiritual life.

   ______ impacted by my relationship with money.

3. I am comfortable when others deal with financial matters.

   True ______ False ______

   Describe how your response impacts your actions or leadership.

4. What experiences or beliefs have shaped my understanding of financial stewardship?
5. What are my personal stewardship practices? My experience with tithing?
6. Stewardship of my personal finances is vital to my spiritual journey.

   True ______ False ______

   Describe how this response impacts my actions or leadership.

7. I have a will and estate plan, and my executor and family know where it is and how to get it when needed.

   True ______ False ______

8. What is the greatest obstacle to effective and joyful stewardship in my life at this moment?

WORKSHEET 3. Personal Values Reflection

Whether you regularly talk about money or are having your first conversation with family, friends, or colleagues, each time you share your values and personal history, you will also clarify your goals.

1. Consider your first job or experience being paid. What did you do, and what type of experience was this for you? What values did you learn or acquire from this experience? How do these values impact your life, your employment decisions, and your generosity?
2. Consider the terms describing money below. Do they align with your experience and understanding of money? Are our definitions formed by feelings or experiences, or are they based in facts?

Money is:

Symbol	Tool	Source of happiness
No value until used	Source of evil	Currency
Source of inspiration	Stewardship tool	Dangerous topic

3. Now consider these statements and whether you believe they are true or false.
    - The use of money is more important than the amount.
    - Money well spent increases in value.
    - Generous people are happier.
    - The way we give money away impacts the way we receive money.
    - Financial stewardship is a spiritual discipline.
4. What aspects of your financial stewardship are clearer now? What would you like to explore further?

WORKSHEET 4. Money Autobiography

Scripture reminds us that having knowledge doesn't mean we always see clearly. Jesus cautions us to first take the plank out of our own eye to see clearly while removing the speck from our brother's eye (see Matt. 7:5). Our experiences influence our attitude, beliefs, and behaviors regarding money. Before assisting others to grow in their personal stewardship, consider the following aspects of your own journey and life lessons about money.

- Think of your first memory or image of money and the feelings and meanings created.
- Describe your jobs or profession and the values acquired through those experiences.
- Think of a scripture passage about money that has special meaning for you.
- Describe the beliefs, attitudes, and financial behaviors learned through prior life experiences.

Journaling and reflecting on your childhood memories or experiences with money or your jobs and the values learned are meaningful ways to deepen your personal stewardship and generosity. Were you taught to trust that everything will work out or that only hard work pays off? Did you experience God's gifts as abundant or scarce? What incidents or traumas still influence your life today? How do those memories or values affect your choices, decisions, and behaviors today?

Write your money autobiography and share it with family and friends. Save your first autobiography, store it with your will, and review it every five years as a reminder to review and update your will. Discover and celebrate how your honest stories inspire and heal you and others and how we are shaped by our memories and beliefs.

One excellent and comprehensive tool for individual or small-group use is the guide "Writing a Money Autobiography," created by noted stewardship expert the Rev. Dan R. Dick, and available online at: http://doroteos2.com/2015/02/11/money-autobiography/.

WORKSHEET 5. Stewardship Dilemmas of Daily Life

Explore the stewardship implications of decisions we make every day of our lives. Individually or with a group, consider the choices below. Which option demonstrates better stewardship in each person's personal opinion? Be careful; these choices may be more difficult than you think!

- Am I intentional about my personal stewardship or do I put it off?
- Should the roof be repaired and replaced? What is the timeline? Who is in charge?
- Should we carpool or drive our own cars?
- Which is better: a face-to-face meeting or a conference call?
- Is it more important to fund a mission trip or pay off church debt?
- Is it better to save for our children's education or fund our pension plan?
- Would I buy an expensive coat to wear for several years or a cheap coat each year?
- Should we use disposable paper products or tableware that needs washing for a community dinner?
- Are cloth or plastic disposable diapers better?
- Do I prefer to purchase books or use the library? Which is better?
- Should we use green cleaning products or bleach-based products?
- Is it better to shop at the farmers' market or local grocery store?
- Should we invest with a commercial institution or a faith-based denominational investment agency?
- Do I use credit to get what I want now or save up until I can pay cash?
- Should I increase my giving to missions or enroll at a fitness center?

After some lively conversation, you may discover some common ground within the group.

WORKSHEET 6. Discover Your Gifts Inventory

After spending some time in personal reflection on the following questions, interview friends and church members to explore their personal gifts and generosity motivators. Are your gifts being stewarded well? Are their gifts being stewarded well?

1. What are my favorite spiritual activities or disciplines? Favorite missions?
2. List my current responsibilities or commitments to a church or mission.
3. Do my commitments align with my first two responses? What changes might I consider to match my interests with my commitments?
4. Describe how I define my personal call from God. What missional needs generate the most anger or passion for me? How do I currently live that call? How could I live that call more fully?
5. If my gift would impact a need or mission, what would I be willing to give?
6. Describe my life choices or employment and explore how it aligns with my gifts and call.
7. Think of an award or recognition I received and gifts that were acknowledged. Do I use those gifts in my current commitments? What are some new options I might explore?

List the names of three to five persons I will interview with these questions

Note: For further exploration of spiritual disciplines and stewardship of gif and talents, see *Equipped for Every Good Work* by Barbara Dick and Dan R. Di and its companion website, http://equippedforeverygoodwork.wordpres .com. The online gifts inventory referenced in chapter 3, http://www.umc .org/what-we-believe/spiritual-gifts-online-assessment, was developed fm this resource.

WORKSHEET 7. Financial Accounts Inventory

Assess whether your financial accounts align with your current mission by identifying all accounts and known purposes. Use this chart to review the number, type, and purpose of the relationships your mission has with financial institutions.

1. Identify all accounts held in the name of your mission in any financial institution, including a bank, credit union, investment manager, foundation, or other money manager, including loans. Be sure to identify every fund held in your name.
2. Define the purpose of each account. What were the motivations and beliefs underlying the creation of each account?
3. Is the definition or need for each account still valid at this time?
4. Identify the accounts that best serve the mission purpose and goals today.
5. Identify any recommended changes and report to the Finance Committee for consideration.

Account Name and Number	Institution	Purpose	Description of Costs, Fees, Benefits, and Interest

Note: Th exercise provides some of the financial information needed for the annual audit and r ew.

WORKSHEET 8. Asset Inventory Categories

Stewardship includes management of all assets, including money, property, and valuable items. An asset inventory protects information for future stewards or in the event of catastrophic circumstances. Whether recorded in writing, digitally, or by video, creating an assets inventory may be the only source of information available for insurance claims, reconstruction, or historical recordkeeping. Your asset inventory is a vital stewardship tool.

To create a basic assets inventory, record the information listed below and store the document in a secure location such as a permanent file. Information can be stored in a notebook, filing system, or electronically. Multiple formats provide the greatest protection.

Financial Assets Inventory: Record descriptions of financial assets, including location, any designations or known purposes, donor information, and other important historical information.

Property Inventory: Record descriptions of property, including address, size, infrastructure, description and dates of improvements, facilities and amenities, maintenance dates, location of deed or incorporation papers, purchase price, and other historical information.

Tangible Goods Inventory: Record descriptions of valuable property items, including location, characteristics, purchase date or information about donors, and other important information.

WORKSHEET 9. Assets Inventory Records—Modified Balance Sheet

This worksheet offers more detailed recordkeeping on assets and their present value. Use this worksheet to record information and store in a secure location. For each asset, record the following information: date, value, designation, governed by, and source or donor. Note any changes in status or value each time the inventory is reviewed. Review is recommended annually.

	Date Acquired	Value	Designation	Governed By	Source or Donor
ASSETS (+)					
Real Estate: *buildings, land, rental property, parsonage, etc.*					
Tangible Property: *vehicles, art, media equipment, computer equipment*					
Stocks/Bonds/Mutual Funds					
Investments Cash Value					
Dividends/Interest Income					
Other Assets/Notes Receivable					
Capital Campaign Receivables					
All Bank or Savings Accounts					
Other Assets					
LIABILITIES (-)					
Mortgages					
Loans					
Credit Card Debt					
Assets Loaned to General Fund					
Amount of Tax or Legal Obligations Pending					
Arrearages Due to Conference or Judicatory					
Other Liabilities					
NET WORTH					
TOTAL: Subtract total liabilities from assets					

WORKSHEET 10. Budget-Building Process

Missions seek to budget faithfully. The process below helps Finance Committees and Church Council or Administrative Boards ensure adequate provision for the financial needs to meet the mission's goals and visions. This process builds a budget to fund clear, compelling mission goals. Identifying missional needs during the budget-building process and striving to meet those goals helps finances avoid limiting vision. Money follows mission, especially when it is clearly communicated.

Financial Stewardship Goal

Create an annual budget with approved expenses supported by realistic income projection or a plan to generate sufficient resources to fund the approved missions.

Building a Budget Proposal

The following steps outline a budgetary review process for Finance Committees preparing a budget proposal.

Income Projection: Review the income projection provided by the financial secretary. Review the previous year's actual income records and note any anticipated changes. Create a realistic and reasonable income projection, including some anticipated growth or decline. Multiple projections (for example, a mission maintenance projection and a growth projection) offer both stability and visionary perspectives. Reviewing the past three to five years of income data will offer additional perspectives. Remember the finance mind-set tends to estimate income conservatively. Creating a *manna* budget projection[2] creates space for possibilities to be named and for the Holy Spirit to act in your midst. Take heed; visions are the seeds God plants!

Expense Budget: Create an expense budget by listening to the ministry areas and looking at their activities, goals, and capacity to accomplish their goals. Inviting ministry team and committee input increases their commitment and ownership of the budget planning process, so include ample

---

2 H. H. Morris, *Demystifying the Congregational Budget* (Washington, DC: Alban Institute, Inc., 1988), 3–4.

opportunities for input and listening. Create your expense budget using any of these budget building processes.

- Bottom-Up: Based on the previous year's allocations and actual expenses, thereby holding ministries accountable for their actual activities rather than their plans. Also known as Use it or Lose it.
- Top-Down: By assessing income and distributing funds over each area, often leading to significant compromise, leaving some feeling their work is under-funded or compromised, but stays within a budget limit.
- Zero-Based: With no guarantees based on previous funding, each area sets goals and requests financial support, creating accountability and sometimes unhealthy conflict.
- A combination of some or all of these methods is also possible.

Carryover: Identify end-of-year account balances for operating expense funds, identified as carryover. Carryover funds may be the cash flow reserve and should be disclosed during the budget-setting process.

Budget Proposal: Compare the proposed expense budget to the proposed income budget. What changes have impacted these projections in recent years? Determine if the proposed expense budget is equal to, greater than, or less than the projected income.

Reflection Questions

- Are we comfortable, challenged, or overwhelmed by this budget assessment?
- Does the proposed budget reflect an optimistic, pessimistic, or realistic income projection?
- Does the proposed budget reflect realistic, padded, or austerity spending?
- What training might you and your church staff need?

Finance leaders sometimes lean into pessimistic or conservative income projections and padded expense projections. Is this faithful? Is the vision growth-oriented or conservation- or protection-oriented?

Budget Assessment

Identify the category that matches your budget projection and consider the related questions.

Surplus Budget: This is previous or projected income greater than proposed budget.

- Is income overstated or are expenses understated?
- Create a supplemental mission list so additional income is part of an approved spending plan.
- Create an endowment line to build resources to support future ministry.
- Increase the expense budget to equal the income projection.

Balanced Budget: A budget is balanced when the proposed expense budget equals income projection.

- Is the income estimate realistic?
- Are any major changes in income or expenses likely?
- Does expense budget include all anticipated expenses?
- Are we comfortable or challenged by this budget?

Underfunded Budget: In an underfunded budget, the proposed expense budget is greater than previous income.

- Many underfunded budgets are balanced by year-end giving or use of accumulated assets or reserves. Has this been disclosed to donors? This budget rescuing eventually erodes trust.
- What types of giving opportunities are offered or could be expanded?
- Does the Finance Committee have a proposal to generate sufficient income to fund the ministry of the church described in the proposed budget?
- If yes, present and approve the plan before adopting the expense budget.
- If no, ask the Finance Committee to create a plan before adopting the budget. Charge Conferences should not adopt a budget without a plan for funding the approved expenses. The plan should include consideration of giving opportunities currently offered and new income opportunities to explore before considering cutting expenses. Do not adopt an unfunded budget without a plan to monitor and adjust during the year!

WORKSHEET 11. Financial Report Review

Note: The figures below are for example only.

	Actual Year-to-Date	Budget Total	Budget Year-to- Date (50%)	YTD % Actual
Income				
Offerings	$60,500	$120,000	$60,000	50%
Monthly Dinners	$3,100	$10,000	$5,000	31%
Investments	$1,200	$4,000	$2,000	30%
Weddings	$1,000	$1,000	$500	100%
Building Users		$20,000	$10,000	0%
Carryover	$1,000	$1,000	$500	100%
Income Total	$66,800	$156,000	$78,000	43%
Expenses				
Worship	$180	$200	$100	90%
Programs	$900	$700	$350	129%
Property	$6,400	$12,400	$6,200	52%
Missions	$1,000	$2,000	$1,000	50%
Personnel	$37,400	$75,000	$37,500	50%
Insurance and Benefits	$12,000	$25,000	$12,500	48%
Maintenance	$8,000	$11,000	$5,500	73%
Apportionments	$11,000	$23,000	$11,500	48%
Expenses Total	$78,880	$149,300	$74,650	53%
Balance (deficit)	($10,080)	$6,700	$3,350	-150%
Faithful Funds Bank (Operations)				
Beginning Balance	$18,870			
Ending Balance	$8,700			
Designated Funds	$4,800			

1. What do the "Actual" column and the bank account balance reveal?
2. How much of the total budget period is reported in this example?
3. What is the difference between the budget projection year-to-date and the actual year-to-date balance?
4. What are the accomplishments and the challenges revealed in this budget?
5. Are there any outstanding financial obligations due to others at this time?
6. How would you describe the overall financial health suggested by this report?

WORKSHEET 12. Multiple Spigots Inventory

Complete the chart below to identify giving opportunities currently provided for donors wishing to express their generosity through your mission work. Then review whether the giving methods currently used meet the missional needs in your community. Should you explore other giving methods?

Giving Method	How Invite/Receive	Frequency	Impact/Publicity/Affirmation

WORKSHEET 13. Giving Opportunities Plan

Kennon Callahan[3] introduced this framework of giving opportunities. Study how they complement one another and the number of times these opportunities are offered, and consider two suggestions for expanding his recommendations. After studying these categories, review your responses in **Worksheet 12** for new missional giving opportunities. Record your plans to implement more giving opportunities to support your missions on the chart below.

Type of Gifts	**Purpose Examples**	**Frequency**
Weekly offerings	Operations/missions	52 times per year
Special offerings	Special needs: house fire, homelessness	3 to 6 per year or more
Missional offerings	Projects: Habitat, Heifer, UMCOR	2 to 4 per year or more
Community worship experiences/offerings	Focus on the neighborhood, strangers, or newcomers in community	6 times plus Christmas and Easter
Special projects giving/capital campaigns	Address higher cost projects	every 2 to 3 years

Giving Opportunity Expansion Plan	**Purpose**	**When**	**Who Will Lead or Ask?**

3 Kennon Callahan, *Giving and Stewardship in an Effective Church* (San Francisco, CA: HarperSan-Francisco, 1992), 49–59.

WORKSHEET 14. Gift Record Tracking Template

Keep information stored with permanent records in a secure location, with a backup copy at another location.

Name of Donor: ______________________________

Donor Contact Info (Address/Email/Phone): ______________________________

Secondary Contact Person: ______________________________

Date of Gift: ______________________________

Gift Description: ______________________________

Understood Intent of Gift: ______________________________

Check One: ____Restricted by Donor ____Unrestricted

Proposed Restrictions on Use: *(The donor will not be able to revise restrictions or influence use of funds after they are accepted.)*

To Be Deposited in:

_____ Current Fund Name:

_____ New Fund *(adopted by Church Council/Board after Trustees review and make recommendation)*

_____ Memorial Fund

_____ Operating Expenses Fund/Account

_____ Endowment Fund *(verify any donor restrictions)*

Trustees Recommendation: ______________________________

Charge Conference Action and Date: ______________________________

Communication with Donor: ______________________________

Acknowledgment Letter (Date Sent): ______________________________

Verification of Purpose and Location of Funds (Date Sent): ______________________________

Follow-Up Communications and Updates (Dates Sent) ______________________________

WORKSHEET 15. Fundraising Quiz

Circle the letter corresponding to the type of fundraising vehicle that best matches the description provided.

Description	Pledge Drive	Capital Campaign	Endow-ment Fund
1. Conducted every year	A	B	C
2. Once established, serves as an opportunity for donors with assets	A	B	C
3. Special purpose drive for about 3 to 5 years	A	B	C
4. Usually funded by cash flow income	A	B	C
5. Prepares for the future	A	B	C
6. Supports annual operations budget	A	B	C
7. A specific large commitment of funds	A	B	C
8. Can be funded by "sacrificial" giving	A	B	C
9. Contributions only from individu-als' accumulated assets are appropriate	A	B	C
10. Stewardship education can positively influence	A	B	C

ANSWERS: 1-A, 2-C, 3-B, 4-A, 5-C, 6-A, 7-A, 8-B, 9-C, 10-ABC

WORKSHEET 16. Budget Balancing Options

This worksheet generates possibilities for resolving a budget gap. Identify a range of options for creating a rebalanced budget. The purpose of this exercise is to clarify financial options and current reality.

Verify Anticipated Need

1. Reduction in anticipated income ____________________
2. Unanticipated expenses ____________________

Total unfunded needs ____________________

Assess Accessible Resources

1. Cash reserves held in bank accounts ____________________
2. Savings or designated reserves ____________________
3. Funds held in CDs or investment accounts ____________________

Total Accessible Resources ____________________

Based on the data above, consider a variety of options focusing on expanding resources before reducing the budget. Review chapter 5 and worksheet 13 for your Giving Opportunities Plan. List all ideas generated without assessment or judgment as to their potential or appropriateness at this time.

Options to Expand Resources

1. ____________________
2. ____________________
3. ____________________
4. ____________________
5. ____________________
6. ____________________

Action Steps

1. Select the top three giving options, including when to implement, who is responsible, and the financial goals assigned to each strategy. Schedule an assessment time to evaluate progress.
2. Identify any cost-saving measures to implement as part of your plan.
3. Identify any asset liquidating options to be considered if needed.
4. Present plan to Finance Committee and church leadership for approval and implementation.
5. Pray and trust God. Take action and remain positive!

WORKSHEET 17. Stewardship Assessment

The following characteristics of culture and stewardship directly impact the financial health of your missions. Consider these characteristics and activities in your setting to affirm healthy practices or to identify areas for growth.

Step One: In each category, rank items on a sliding scale from 1 to 5, where 1 represents opportunity for growth and 5 represents area of strength.

Mission Awareness: Members know about the missions supported and their purpose.

______Opportunities other than the weekly offering are provided for support of selected missions projects.

______Results of special mission project giving is reported immediately.

______New mission activities start each year.

______All members and friends are encouraged to actively participate in at least one mission project a year beyond providing financial support.

______Fundraising efforts are calendared and coordinated through the Finance Committee/Church Council for scheduling and timing of projects.

______**Category Subtotal**

Giving: Pledged or reliable giving contributions support at least 65 percent of the total planned expenditures (75–85 percent recommended). Giving increases when:

______Opportunities are provided for members to explore and learn about personal finance management, tithing, and pledging.

______Members know who to ask about church finances or special gifts and giving ideas.

______Pledge or commitment opportunities are provided year-round.

______The pastor has knowledge of member giving patterns.

______Generosity is celebrated and integrated into year-round worship through liturgy and preaching.

______**Category Subtotal**

Budgeting: Budget process is participatory and focused on cooperation and mutual support among ministry areas.

______Finance Committee understands its responsibility for funding proposed ministry.

______Ministry is proposed first, and then funding is explored.
______Planning process includes full disclosure of all resources and assets.
______Narrative or storytelling supplements the line item budget.
______A funded budget is proposed each year.

______**Category Subtotal**

Policies: Written policies guide fund management and distribution for all special funds, such as endowments, memorials, scholarships, and building use by members and by community groups.

______Adopted policies are reviewed and updated at least every three years, preferably every year.
______Communication about gifts to enduring funds is provided at least quarterly.
______Communication about planned giving and gifts from assets or estates is provided at least quarterly.

______**Category Subtotal**

Step Two

Add the category subtotals and record the overall total here:_______.

- **18–34** indicates lots of room to grow.
- **35–60** suggests many opportunities for improvement.
- **61–90** indicates good practices upon which to build.
- **91–105** indicates you are ready to be a role model for others!

Step Three

The assessment may have surfaced multiple next steps. To ensure follow-through and focus on achievable goals, select six areas to focus on this year to strengthen stewardship effectiveness. Identify three Strengths to Celebrate and three Opportunities to Develop using the chart below. Include supporting these strengths and opportunities in your year-round stewardship goals this year.

Strengths to Celebrate	Opportunities to Develop into Strengths
1.	1.
2.	2.
3.	3.

WORKSHEET 18. Pastoral Role Expectations

Pastors approach leadership with a wide range of expectations about their role in financial management and stewardship. Prayerfully consider the questions below and identify the conversations needed to build a culture of generosity and transparency about money and its role in your mission. Past experiences will shape expectations and perspectives for both pastors and laity. Listening to one another's responses is the most important part of this exercise.

Questions

1. Is your pastor encouraged or discouraged from talking about stewardship and money?
2. Are you, as pastor, comfortable or uncomfortable talking and preaching about stewardship and money?
3. What are the biblical messages that influence your church's relationship with money?
4. Would people support or discourage the pastor from talking about stewardship and money?
5. What values or historical experiences contribute to your own relationship with money?
6. What is our understanding of the relationship between spiritual formation and generosity?
7. What action steps will create more comfort and encouragement for the pastor and for the members?

Action Steps

Identify three or four action steps emerging from this conversation. Action steps may be personal commitments or group commitments; they may include follow-up conversations or plans for worship or education projects. Your action steps need to fit your current ministry reality. Set a timeline for next steps to ensure follow-through.

WORKSHEET 19. Pastoral Stewardship of Giving—Culture-Shift Process

Assuming the responsibility for stewarding donor giving information could be a simple request in some faith communities. In other cases, this will require a more intentional change process. The steps outlined here offer guidance for understanding, planning, and implementing a transition from not knowing donors' giving information to stewarding that information professionally.

Culture Shift

Any leader who has implemented a culture shift knows the process is both life-giving and risky. Many people are risk-averse. Because pastoral stewardship of giving information may require acknowledging and shifting long-standing cultural norms, some will experience mild tremors while others may feel earthquakes.

First, remember some leaders already steward giving information in ways that enhance ministry and generosity. Pastors already stewarding donor information professionally offer hope and guidance to others. Because stewardship and financial management education is quite limited in pastoral education, this aspect of leadership is likely to be unfamiliar territory.

When changing the culture, remember the following guiding principle: the privilege of stewarding giving information is sacred work, motivated by the desire to provide appropriate pastoral care for each person. For some, this aligns well with their vision for leadership. If you are a pastoral leader whose pastoral care has been impaired by financial secrecy, or if you are trying to decide how to move in this direction or if you find your leadership being challenged, consider these preparatory steps. Successful pastoral leaders carefully assess readiness, their personal gifts, and the cultural context when navigating change.

Step One. Recognize Your Personal History and Relationship with Money

- How honest are you with yourself about your relationship with money?
- Are you early in your ministry in this setting or has trust been established?
- Are you trustworthy and seen as trustworthy by others?

- Are you known to hold confidential information professionally: medical, relational, or financial?
- Are you in financial distress yourself? If needed, seek counsel and personal support.

Leaders cannot lead others into generosity they have not yet discovered and practiced themselves. While you may begin the conversation if your personal finances are stressed, the journey is harder, and your anxiety is likely to leak out and trigger anxiety in others.

Warning! Simply declaring the authority to steward giving and demanding information typically triggers resistance, which reduces generosity and trust rather than strengthening it. Prayerfully consider this question: How do I steward this responsibility with grace rather than with power?

Step Two. Understand the Culture and Context

- Are the finance leaders confident and competent or worried and anxious?
- Are there historical violations of trust or unhealed trauma related to the pastoral role, or past or present unresolved conflict that change might exacerbate?
- Is financial information currently guarded or openly shared? What about the budget, total assets, debt, and audits?
- Is the information that is shared clear or confusing? Has the community talked about financial transparency in the past? How did that go?
- What is their history with change? Are the people committed to growth and open to the changes that will be required?

Leaders' responses to these questions offer indicators of the readiness or roadblocks in the system. Some other trust issues may need to be resolved first and will impact the pace and timing of your communication and options.

Step Three. Plan Your Process

A pastor's personal readiness to lead and level of clarity about culture and history will have a significant impact on how the stewardship of giving information is introduced and implemented. What works in one setting could be counterproductive in another setting. What is the right audience for this conversation? The Finance Committee, Pastor Parish Relations Committee, Church Council, Charge Conference? Remember what you have learned about this faith community.

Decide what your next steps will be; write them down and pray for courage to lead. Share your plan with a small group of people you trust. Present your plan clearly and boldly, and then listen. Collaboratively identify who needs to be part of the conversation, including where resistance is most likely. Remember, resistance is almost always an excuse for limiting our generosity and may be an important gateway to greater pastoral care. Be prepared to reach out rather than withdraw.

Remember your motivation is to strengthen your ministry and the church's mission goals. In many cases, just asking will be sufficient. Most important, just begin.

Ongoing Professional Stewardship

Pastoral leadership requires accepting people where they are, cultivating generosity effectively by using data rather than guessing, sharing information about giving options suitable for donors' life situations, and recognizing appropriately all gifts as acts of generosity made possible by God. Pastoral leadership may include sharing your story more openly so that others might benefit from the shared struggle with our consumer culture and grow closer together. The first step in unmasking a culture that discourages generosity may be your own testimonial.

How will you continue to manage the relational and pastoral authority of affirming, challenging, and coaching members toward the joy of generosity? How will you prepare to coach people through the spiritual journey of recovery from money addiction and trauma as both individuals and a church? Wise pastoral leadership can offer healing and rebuild trust when disappointing things happen.

None of us ventures into new territory alone. Successful leaders take others with them. Share your experience with colleagues and friends judiciously; be careful to maintain appropriate boundaries. Find ways to contribute and equip church members and leaders to give joyfully. Know that God is present. Who will you take on this journey with you?

WORKSHEET 20. Communication and Celebration Goals

Many groups and leaders contribute to a church's communications culture. Gather a team of leaders representing different aspects of your mission to explore opportunities for improving communication. Use the questions below to generate ideas and action steps.

Questions

1. How is financial information communicated about your mission? Describe the tone. Is it appreciative, anxious, inspiring, fear-provoking?
2. Share examples of financial information communication that inspires you.
3. Describe how donors are affirmed and thanked. List ways and times donors can be thanked.
4. How do you celebrate generosity? How do you identify people to thank?
5. What missional activities and stories can your mission celebrate?
6. List your mission activities. How are they shared and celebrated?
7. How often do you offer missional stories or testimonials? In what context? In what setting?
8. How can your affirmation and communication activities increase?

Action Plan

Describe the action steps you will implement to increase affirmation and communications about missional activities and service to known and unknown neighbors. List three to five action steps, including due dates and who is responsible for implementation.

Action	When	Leader
1. ____________________	__________	__________
2. ____________________	__________	__________
3. ____________________	__________	__________
4. ____________________	__________	__________
5. ____________________	__________	__________

WORKSHEET 21. Liturgical Year Stewardship Framework

Use the following principles and questions to build stewardship components into worship liturgy.[4]

Stewardship Principles

God owns it all. What are we freely giving or tithing?

God claims us as stewards. What are we caring for and creating?

God's priorities are those in need. Whose needs are we meeting?

Today matters! What are we doing now?

Personal Reflections throughout the Year

What am I giving, supporting, and expressing thankfulness for?

What gifts does God seek from me to create God's vision?

Whose life is better because of me?

Liturgical Seasons Reflections

Advent

Is our giving a preparation for Jesus?

Is our giving compassionate toward creation?

Does our giving affirm God's priorities?

Christmas and Epiphany

God gives! That is our present.

How do we care for God's child and creation?

With whom to do we share this present?

Lent

How do we acknowledge God's ownership?

Search deeper for our gifts.

Seek the hurting, making room in your heart.

Easter

God has a master plan!

Humanity connects with the divine through Jesus.

The kingdom is open to all: the poor, those who suffer, those with limited abilities, and others.

Pentecost 1

God intended diversity.

God uses all of us; all of us can be good stewards.

God's love is for everyone, bridging all differences.

Pentecost 2

Harvest belongs to God.

God's love multiplies our gifts.

Reaping and gleaning: Who receives the fruit?

---

4 Adapted from content created for the United Methodist Foundation of New England (UMFNE). Used with permission.

WORKSHEET 22. Year-Round Stewardship Planning Calendar

A year-round stewardship plan can include a preaching series, planned giving education, children and youth activities, personal finance classes, communication strategies, celebration of mission, and liturgical season themes. Use the calendar template below to build your year-round stewardship plan; note that several projects are pre-filled for your convenience.

Year-Round Stewardship Planning Calendar			
Annual Theme and Scripture: Commitment Sunday Date:			
JANUARY Letters to donors for previous year gifts	**FEBRUARY**	**MARCH** Personal finance or debt workshop	**LENT** Lenten study with stewardship/ planned-giving focus/mission funding goal
APRIL Quarterly statement to donors with good news from pastor	**MAY** Vacation letter with envelopes for summer gifts, or electronic giving invitation	**JUNE** Mission project	**PENTECOST**
JULY Quarterly statement to donors with good news from pastor	**AUGUST**	**SEPTEMBER** Start publicity for commitment campaign	**Commitment** Process preparations
OCTOBER Quarterly statement to donors with good news from pastor Commitment campaign: 3–4 weeks	**NOVEMBER** Mail year-end gifts letters	**DECEMBER**	**ADVENT** Alternative giving project for a designated mission

WORKSHEET 23. Testimonial Preparation Tips

You have been asked to share a stewardship and generosity testimonial. This outline[5] offers tips and inspiration for your planning. Because generosity has already warmed your heart, telling your story is a gift to God that will inspire others. Consider these steps as you create your testimonial story.

1. Pray and reflect on scripture. Listen for the assurance and biblical texts that speak to you.
2. Think about your experience with God's generosity, presence, and assurance in your life.
3. Identify times when your faith and confidence in God's presence and plan were tested.
4. Acknowledge God's blessings and your experience with stewardship and generosity.
5. Reflect on any life-changing events.
6. Name and give thanks for those who inspired or mentored you.
7. Has your stewardship commitment been challenged? How did you overcome challenges?
8. Identify the spiritual and personal changes in your life resulting from your stewardship and your response to God's generosity.

As you draft your narrative, use an outline or a script format using the following elements.

- Introduce yourself.
- Share your understanding of stewardship and God's generosity.
- Share your personal story.
- Invite others to experience the joy you have found through your generosity and how it is available to all people.

Important points include the principle of "first fruits" giving, our need to be generous and give thanks, and the joy and fulfillment we receive from God when we express our gratitude and trust in God. Give thanks to God for the opportunity to be a blessing and inspiration to others.

Pray and share your story!

---

5 Adapted from "Preparation for Lay Witness Presentation," in *Stewardship Sourcebook* (New Canaan, CT: Parish Publishing Inc. LLC, 2014), 41–42; www.parishpublishing.org.

WORKSHEET 24. Narrative Budget

A picture is worth a thousand words, and a narrative budget presentation converts your line item budget into an inspiring visual. With creative and inspiring descriptions and stories about your mission, a narrative budget can become an informative brochure or presentation. In reality, you are creating a marketing and evangelism tool.

Transforming your line item budget into a mission-oriented story requires a moderately simple math exercise, most easily managed using a spreadsheet program such as Excel. Work with a small team of leaders, including Finance and Stewardship Committee members, staff, a skilled writer, and, if available, a graphic artist because your budget story or pie chart is supplemented with pictures of people and ministries as well as testimonials. Most important, have fun, and celebrate all God is doing through your mission.

Step 1. Select four to six categories that encompass your ministry activities. In most settings, worship, education, mission, fellowship, and pastoral care will work. Select categories that fit your ministry context. Do *not* create categories for administration, facilities, debt, or staff; these are distributed over the broader categories. This document promotes your mission; it is not intended to replace the accounting tools used by committees. Too many categories will diminish the impact of your chart results. Remember your audience is your community, not committee members.

Step 2. Using a spreadsheet version of the current or recent line item budget, create one column for each category. Then, assign percentages representing the approximate amount of each line item for each category. Administration and infrastructure costs (e.g., utilities, staff, debt) are distributed across the categories. Some items will clearly belong in one column, while others will fit into a number of categories. For example, the choir director may fall 100 percent in the worship category. Or, that job might also include team building and even pastoral care, so worship might receive 90 percent, and fellowship and pastoral care 5 percent each. While a time analysis would generate much more detailed results, usually a rough estimate is sufficient. Note in the example on the following pages that percentages in the property line item are given in the total line because the percentage distribution for each of the lines is the same. The process of assigning these percentages has the potential to generate some challenging reflection questions. Your decisions about the distribution of the pastor's time and whether the building is used all week long or just on Sundays will help sort out what set of percentages feels acceptable.

Line Item Distribution across Ministry Categories (as percentages)

	Budget	Worship	Mission	Education	Community	Pastoral Care
Administration						
Copier	$500	25%	10%	25%	20%	20%
Postage	$120			20%	60%	20%
Supplies	$750	25%	10%	25%	20%	20%
Stewardship	$1,000	10%	20%	10%	50%	10%
Property		25%	10%	25%	20%	20%
Maintenance	$4,000					
Electricity	$8,000					
Insurance	$14,000					
Program						
Worship supplies	$500	100%				
Flowers	$350	80%			20%	
Youth	$1,500			100%		
VBS	$1,400			80%	20%	
Coffee/Fellowship	$200				100%	
Mission						
Community Meals	$2,000		50%		50%	
Apportionments	$22,000		100%			
Discretionary	$1,500		100%			
Habitat for Humanity	$3,000		100%			

	Budget	Worship	Mission	Education	Community	Pastoral Care
Personnel						
Pastor, includes benefits	$72,000	20%	20%	20%	20%	20%
Christian Ed Dir.	$22,000	10%		70%	20%	
Admin. Asst.	$14,000	40%		20%	40%	
Music Dir.	$16,000	90%			10%	
Organist	$14,000	100%				
Custodian	$6,500	40%	10%	40%	5%	5%
Childcare Provider	$5,600	90%			10%	

Step 3. Create another set of columns with the same categories (see below).

Step 4. Multiply each line item's budget amount by the percentage assigned to calculate the dollar amount of each line item assigned to each category. For example, all $14,000 for the Organist was allocated to worship (100%), so the category dollar amount would be $14,000. The $2,000 budgeted for community meals would be $1,000 fellowship and $1,000 mission because 50 percent was assigned to each category. Note that the property line summarizes the distribution for the line items below it because those line items were all given the same percentage distribution.

Results of Line Item Distribution over Categories

	Worship	Mission	Education	Community	Pastoral Care
Administration					
Copier	$125	$50	$125	$100	$100
Postage			$24	$72	$72
Supplies	$188	$75	$188	$150	$150
Stewardship	$100	$200	$100	$500	$500

	Worship	Mission	Education	Community	Pastoral Care
Property	$6,500	$2,600	$6,500	$5,200	$5,200
Maintenance					
Electricity					
Insurance					
Program					
Worship supplies	$500				
Flowers	$280			$70	
Youth			$1,500		
VBS			$1,120	$280	
Coffee/Fellowship				$200	
Mission					
Meals		$1,000		$1,000	
World Missions		$22,000			
Discretionary		$1,500			
Habitat for Humanity		$3,000			
Personnel					
Pastor	$14,400	$14,400	$14,400	$14,400	$14,400
Christian Ed Dir.	$2,200		$15,400	$4,400	$4,400
Admin. Asst.	$5,600		$2,800	$5,600	$5,600
Music Dir.	$14,400			$1,600	$1,600
Organist	$14,000				
Custodian	$2,600	$650	$2,600	$325	$325
Childcare Provider	$5,040			$560	$560
TOTAL	$65,933	$45,475	$44,757	$34,457	$20,299
Percentage of Budget	28%	19%	19%	15%	9%

Step 5. Total the amounts now recorded in each category and divide into the total budget amount, generating the percentage of the total budget allocated to each of the selected categories. The resulting percentage (Percentage of Budget row) indicates the portion of the total budget supporting that category. For example, the Education column represents 19 percent of the total budget, including materials and supplies, plus a portion of the staff, building, and maintenance costs.

Step 6. Create a chart to show categories visually. (Excel offers a simple mechanism for this.) A pie chart is an effective visual depicting categories in an attractive and inviting format. Samples are available online. A pie chart, labeled with percentages or dollar amounts, or both, orients people to your missional priorities. After perfecting labels and colors, a pie chart can be pasted into another document.

Sample Pie Chart Created Using Excel

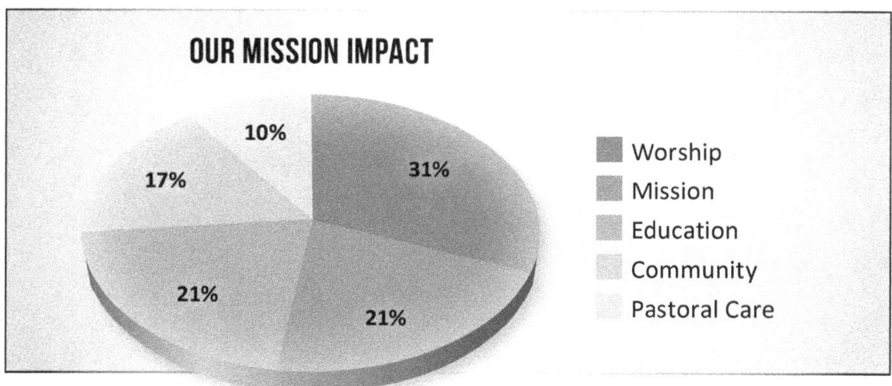

Step 7. Write ministry category descriptions, and be sure to include activities, special events, and programs. This provides inspiring and helpful information to readers. Illustrate with inspirational stories to show how your mission and ministry impacts and changes lives. Use pictures and videos of your church members and donors to show ministry in action. Then invite others into the vision by identifying several exciting emerging missions. Plant ideas and sow the seeds of what is possible as resources increase.

Step 8. A good design eye is helpful, and many formats—one page, booklet, tri-fold brochures, bulletin insert, slide presentations (such as

PowerPoint)—are all effective. Place a few copies of the line item budget in the office and bring them to Charge Conference and leadership gatherings for those who ask for them.

A pastor told me this story. One of his church members was disgruntled about being asked each year to donate money for a particular mission in Africa. Her comment was, "Why are we helping people so far away, when there is so much to be done here?" Her attitude also affected others in the congregation, until one Sunday morning during worship, the mission leader showed a video of the woman's granddaughter teaching African children from that mission to play soccer. From then on, it was a completely different story. Her own granddaughter was making a difference; the grandmother was so proud and now willing to help fund that ministry.

Help make your budget a stewardship, evangelism, and marketing tool to communicate the impact and exciting message of your mission. A narrative budget is useful during a pledge or commitment campaign, and it is useful for ongoing stewardship education or as part of a visitor information packet. Promote generosity by celebrating your mission activities! Watch the energy grow.

CPSIA information can be obtained
at www.ICGtesting.com
Printed in the USA
LVHW032345290321
682892LV00013B/1073